HAL LEONARD
DRUMSET METHOD

COMPLETE EDITION

Contains Books 1 and 2 Bound

MW00823630

BY KENNAN WYLIE

WITH GREGG BISSONETTE

PLAYBACK+

Speed • Pitch • Balance • Loop

To access audio, video, and extra content visit:
www.halleonard.com/mylibrary

Enter Code
1585-0741-2959-8180

ISBN 978-1-4950-8334-1

HAL•LEONARD®

7777 W. BLUEMOUND RD. P.O. BOX 13819 MILWAUKEE, WI 53213

In Australia Contact:
Hal Leonard Australia Pty. Ltd.
4 Lentara Court
Cheltenham, Victoria, 3192 Australia
Email: ausadmin@halleonard.au

Copyright © 2017 by HAL LEONARD LLC
International Copyright Secured   All Rights Reserved

No part of this publication may be reproduced in any form or by any means without
the prior written permission of the Publisher.

Visit Hal Leonard Online at **www.halleonard.com**

BOOK 1 CONTENTS

BOOK 2 CONTENTS

◉ INTRODUCTION

Welcome to the **Complete Edition** of the *Hal Leonard Drumset Method*! This comprehensive beginner's pack includes **Books 1 and 2**, plus all of their accompanying audio tracks, video lessons, and downloadable practice materials. Book 1 is designed to help the beginning drummer develop hand and foot technique, read music, play basic rock beats and fills, develop coordination and independence, play basic jazz patterns, and much more. Book 2 explores four-limb independence through the use of ostinato patterns, syncopated grooves, fills, and beat combination patterns. Basic chart reading will be covered, including articulations, musical symbols, and ensemble figures, along with brush playing and even how to build a basic drum solo. Musical styles such as funk, country, hip-hop, soca, Afro-Cuban, Brazilian, and more are also introduced.

ABOUT THE AUDIO AND VIDEO

To access the audio and video files that accompany this book, simply visit **www.halleonard.com/mylibrary** and enter the code found on page 1. From here you can download or stream all of the audio and video files.

Each main exercise and song in this book includes two audio tracks:

1. A **demonstration track** that includes the notated drum part so you can hear how the example is supposed to sound.

2. A **play-along track** of the same example *without* the drums, so you can practice it along with the backing instruments.

The audio tracks for each exercise continue on a loop for approximately three minutes so you have plenty of time to listen or play along. When there are multiple lines within one exercise, the band will continue playing through them without any breaks.

Video lessons are also included, featuring drum master Gregg Bissonette! Gregg will demonstrate introductory concepts, song examples, and techniques throughout the book.

Examples including audio and/or video are marked with icons throughout:

ABOUT THE DOWNLOADABLE PDF

In addition to the audio and video, you also have access to even more content: a downloadable PDF containing further drum exercises for study and practice. You can download the PDF using the same access code and website mentioned above.

HOW TO PRACTICE

1. **Go Slowly:** Learn new beats and stickings at a slow tempo.

2. **Use a Metronome:** Always use a metronome to reinforce good time-keeping.

3. **Be Repetitive:** Each line should be repeated up to 10 times, at a minimum, to develop muscle memory.

4. **Stay Relaxed:** Avoid tension in the grip, the feet, and the body.

5. **Record Yourself:** Record yourself playing and self-evaluate what you hear.

PARTS OF THE DRUMSET

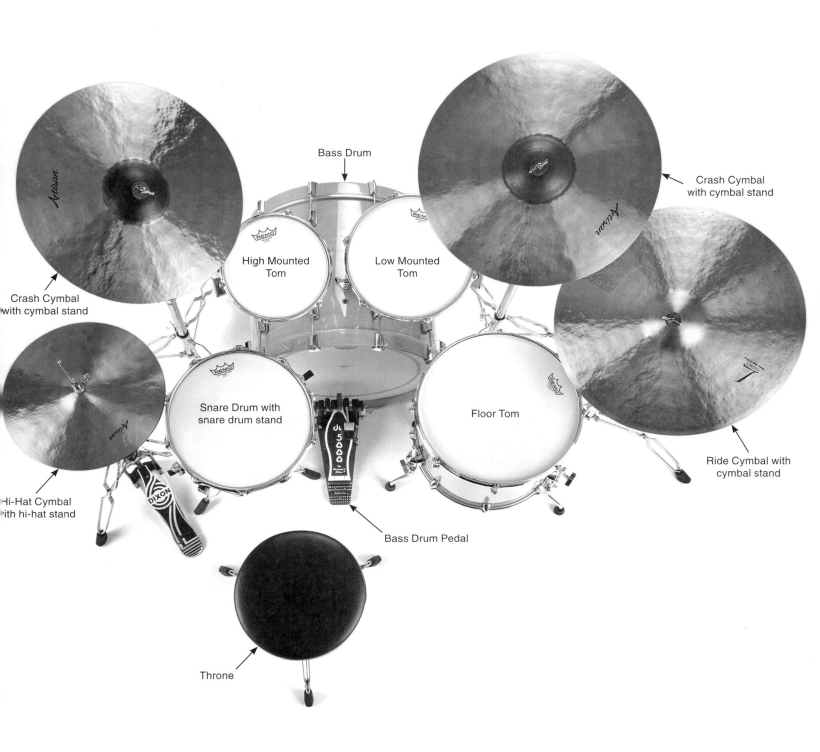

Bass Drum

Crash Cymbal
with cymbal stand

Crash Cymbal
with cymbal stand

High Mounted
Tom

Low Mounted
Tom

Hi-Hat Cymbal
with hi-hat stand

Snare Drum with
snare drum stand

Floor Tom

Ride Cymbal with
cymbal stand

Bass Drum Pedal

Throne

SETTING UP YOUR DRUMSET

The drumset is a very personalized instrument to arrange. What works for one drummer may not exactly work for the next drummer. The bigger the drumset does *not* mean the better the drummer. The most important thing to remember is to use the right equipment for the style of music you are playing. However, there are some common approaches that all drummers share when arranging their drumset.

Throne (Stool)

Proper positioning of the drum throne can have a great effect on the drummer's balance, as well as foot technique. Both the height and distance from the drums can impact the drummer's performance. Some players sit with their legs almost parallel to the floor while others keep their legs slightly above parallel to the floor with the heels just below the knees. Your feet should feel comfortable on the pedals. The drummer should experiment until maximum relaxation and efficiency is achieved. Avoid using chairs or stools that do not adjust.

Snare Drum

The snare drum should be positioned in a way that does not interfere with the proper alignment of the forearms and hands. Matched grip players (see "Grips and Strokes" on page 8) usually keep the snare drum flat, while traditional grip players might use a slight downward tilt. The snare drum should stay a few inches above knee level.

Bass Drum/Hi-Hat

After the snare drum is set up between your legs, the bass drum and hi-hat pedals can be placed on the floor. The bass drum should be positioned just below, or in front of, your knee. The hi-hat pedal should be within easy reach of your hi-hat playing foot (typically the left foot). Once a relaxed position has been set with the feet over the pedals, you can now slide the bass drum in to fit your setup. Some drummers may choose to start with the foot pedals and bass drum first, adding the snare after. The primary goal is to set things up consistently for a relaxed playing position.

Mounted Toms

Drummers can use one or more mounted toms (also called "tom-toms"). Try to get them as close to each other without touching, or else they may rattle against each other while playing. The tilt of the toms should be slightly downward towards you. Avoid too much tilt; this can affect the sound due to the angle of the stick striking the tom head.

Floor Tom

The floor tom should be almost the same height as the snare drum. It usually sits with a slight angle towards the drummer. Make sure the right knee has enough room to comfortably use the bass drum pedal without rubbing against the floor tom.

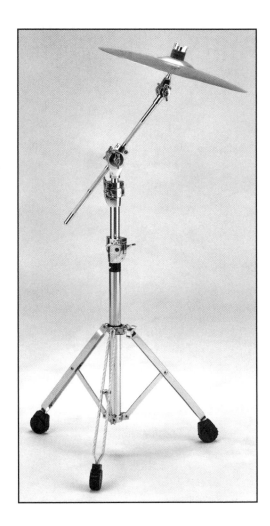

Crash Cymbal

Placement of the crash cymbals may depend on how many you have and the size of the drumset. Usually a crash is placed to the left of the toms. The crash cymbal should be tilted slightly and placed within normal reach so the shaft of the drumstick can strike the edge of the cymbal.

Ride Cymbal

The ride cymbal should be positioned in a way that will allow the drummer to easily reach the stick three to four inches in from the edge of the ride cymbal. This should be achieved without extending the elbow.

PARTS OF THE DRUMSTICK

Drumsticks come in assorted sizes. Some basic sizes to start with are 7A, 5A, and 5B. Use a stick that works best for you.

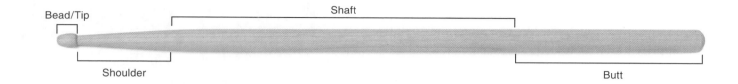

Bead/Tip

Shaft

Shoulder

Butt

PARTS OF THE SNARE DRUM

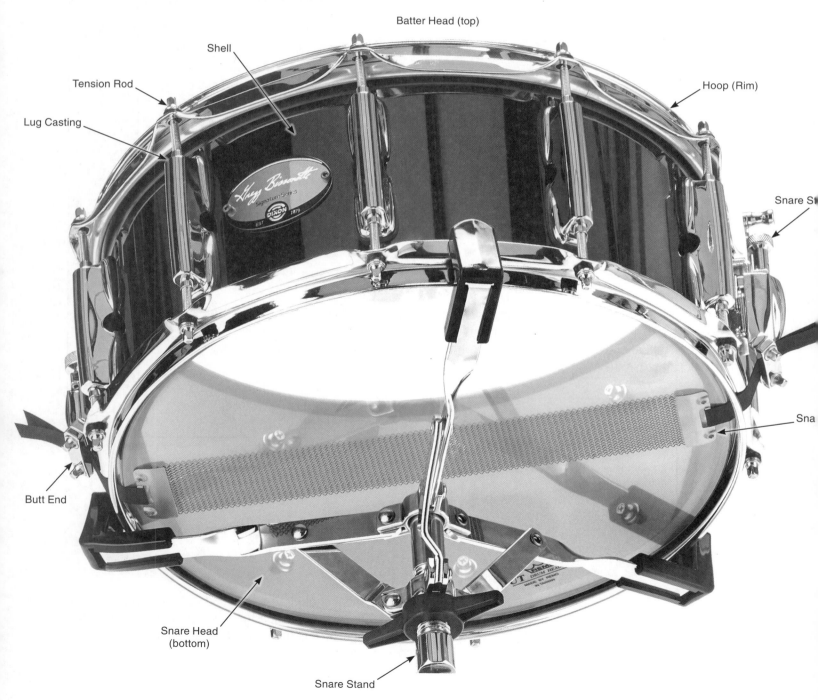

Batter Head (top)

Shell

Tension Rod

Hoop (Rim)

Lug Casting

Snare S

Butt End

Sna

Snare Head
(bottom)

Snare Stand

ADDITIONAL ITEMS

Practice Pad

A practice pad enables a drummer to practice without generating all of the volume of a real drum.

Metronome

A metronome is a device that provides a perfect pulse at any desired tempo.

Ear Buds

Headphones or ear buds can help you hear the click or the music you are playing to at a safe volume level.

Ear Plugs

Ear plugs are the safest method to protect from hearing loss.

CARE OF THE DRUMS

CHANGING THE HEADS

Replacing the top or bottom drumhead is probably the most regular maintenance your drums will require. Carefully loosen each of the tension rods using a drum key. After removing each rod, remove the hoop (rim) and discard the old head. Take some time at this point to use a cloth and wipe any excess dirt from the inside shell. Even check to make sure all of the lug casing screws inside the shell are tightly fastened. Before adding the new head, use a small drop of lubricating oil (like Vaseline) on the threads of each rod. This will help the tension rods stay smooth inside the casings during the tuning of your drum.

TUNING THE SNARE DRUM

The sound and feel of your snare drum will depend upon the tuning. This includes: a) the tension of the drumheads, and b) the tension of the snare strainer. After each rod has been finger tightened, we're now ready to use the drum key. Start with quarter turns; be sure that the same tension is applied to each rod. Always tune in opposite pairs (see diagram below). This will allow the head to stretch evenly. Occasionally tap the head in front of the tension rods and adjust each area as close to the same pitch as possible. The batter (top) head is thicker and can handle a bit more torque than the thinner clear snare (bottom) head.

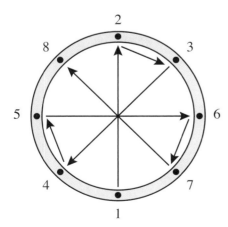

Proper snare tension is another important part of drum tuning. The screw on snare strainer will allow you to tighten or loosen the snares. If the snares are too tight, it will make the drum sound choked. If the snares are too loose, it will cause them to vibrate. The performer must use his or her own discretion on how to reach the desired sound.

▣ GRIPS AND STROKES

MATCHED GRIP

Of the two main grips, **matched grip** is the more basic. The right and left hand should look and move identically.

- Place the stick in between the thumb and index finger, about four to five inches from the butt end of the stick. The pivot point between the index finger and the thumb is referred to as the **fulcrum** (left photo below). Another option is to have the fulcrum between the middle finger and thumb (right photo below) for more of a loose feel. This very important part of the grip is responsible for control. It needs to be quite secure. Try marking this point with a piece of tape or a felt pen.

- Keep the thumbs on the side of the stick.

- Keep the tip of the index fingers curved slightly around the stick and not pointed. This will help control.

- Keep the back fingers resting gently on the stick. Avoid hanging them in the air. Also avoid grasping the stick too tightly with the fingers. The stick will not be able to move freely when it needs to (especially when rebounding).

- Where you grip as well as *how* you grip the stick can affect the tone production. Squeezing the stick can "choke" the sound. On the other hand, gripping too loosely can cause control problems.

- The thumbs should almost face each other. This will help keep the back of the hands a bit more flat. Try to keep at least 60 to 70 percent of the back of the hand facing upward (left photo below).

- Avoid air pockets. This occurs when the space between the stick and the index finger and the thumb gets too big.

- Try to keep the sticks positioned close to a 90 degree angle (right photo below). It doesn't have to be exact, but close. Don't hold the sticks too close to each other.

- Try to keep the sticks in the center of the drum or practice pad. Check your sticks to make sure they stay in the same beating area.

 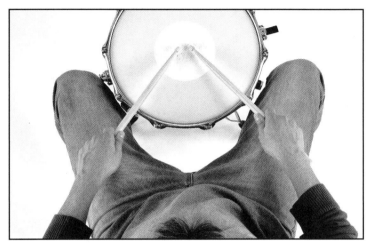

TRADITIONAL GRIP

Traditional grip is the other most common grip. The major difference here is the left-hand position; the right hand is identical to matched grip.

- Place the left stick in the webbing between the thumb and index finger, about four inches from the butt end (left photo below).

- The middle part of the thumb should touch the index finger in between the first and second joints.

- The stick will rest on the third (ring) finger near the inside of the first joint. This third finger serves as a bridge for the grip. The index, third, and fourth fingers should be parallel to each other (right photo below).

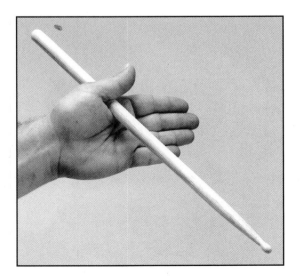 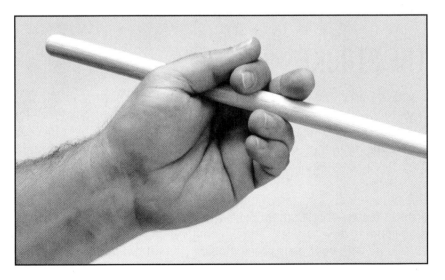

- The pinky finger should be tucked in a position that won't interfere with the third finger. Some people teach curling and pulling back the pinky finger. Whatever you choose, make sure that it does not interfere with the bridge of your grip (left photo below).

- The middle finger curves over the top of the stick. Some people may teach keeping this finger straight up (right photo below).

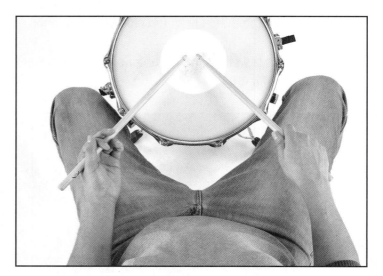

When learning the basic stroke using traditional grip, the right hand acts the same as in matched grip. The left hand, however, is slightly different. Imagine turning a doorknob to get the feel of this wrist action. It should be a very relaxed motion. Start your stroke with the left palm facing inward. As your wrist turns, the inside palm will face upward. The photos below show how you can practice this left-hand wrist motion.

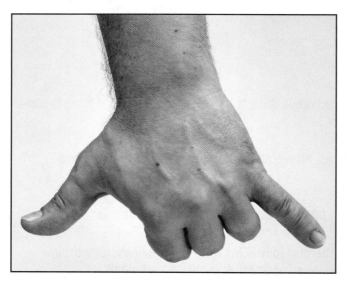
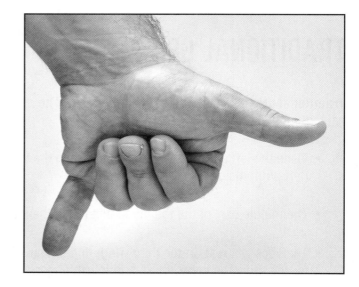

Traditional grip players often tilt the snare drum slightly downward.

THE STROKE

There are only two ways to stroke the drum. The player can either let the stick rebound when it strikes the drum, or it can be controlled (or stopped) by the player as soon as the drum is stroked. You can simplify this by using the terms "rebound" vs. "control." The term you use does not matter, as long as you can readily know and play each.

One of the most important things to achieve when learning to play the snare drum is the art of relaxation. Believe it or not, some people have a very hard time learning how to relax. Try extending your arms straight out in front of your body with your palms facing down (photo). Wiggle your wrist like you are waving "goodbye" (like an infant!). Now put the stick in your hand.

REBOUND STROKE

The **rebound stroke** is a very relaxed natural stroke that tends to produce a more **legato**, or "smooth" sound. Use your wrist and let the stick rebound by itself. Start with the wrist in the "up" position by turning the wrist (left photo below). Imagine throwing the stick towards the drum and letting it come back freely (middle photo below). Avoid pulling the stick back! Use plenty of wrist and avoid jabbing with the forearm. Play with the sticks at a height of at least nine inches above the drumhead. Use more velocity (or speed) for a bigger sound. The left hand in traditional grip turns differently using the same feel (right photo below).

Try the following exercise using a rebound stroke.

TECHNIQUE ▶

The Rebound Stroke (8 on a hand)

R R R R R R R R – L L L L L L L L

Right Stick = R / Left Stick = L

Work on developing consistent strokes and an even sound. Remember to stay relaxed. The stroke is very similar to that of dribbling a basketball. Use your wrist and avoid jabbing with the forearm!

After establishing a consistent grip and hand position, you can really focus on the rebound stroke. This first type of stroke will be used throughout the book as you learn new sticking combinations and new rhythms. The use of arms and fingers for the controlled stroke will gradually be added with the introduction of accents, flams, etc.

CONTROLLED STROKE

The **controlled stroke** requires the player to hold on to the stick a little more tightly. Be careful not to squeeze the stick so tightly that the movement of the stick is stifled. The fulcrum part of the grip is very important in maintaining a solid control point. The controlled stroke is used often with accents and flams. This particular stroke will be covered in more detail later in the book.

LESSON 1: GETTING STARTED

> **QUICK TIP** – Drum rudiments are fundamental sticking patterns that all drummers should know well. Each should be practiced at different tempos and dynamics while playing with a relaxed feel.

Let's get started by doing some basic stick combinations. Remember that the goal here is to strive for consistency in the stroke. The left stick and right stick should produce the same sound. A listener who shuts his eyes should be unable to tell which hand you are using. Things to think about while you play:

- Use your wrist! Really work it out! You will be able to use more wrist at the slower speeds than the faster ones. Strength and flexibility are a very important part of wrist development.

- Watch your sticks! Make sure each stick is raised to the same height. If the sticks don't come back to the same level, there is a greater chance that they will not sound even. It may also affect the steadiness of tempo.

- Check out your hand position frequently. Keep your back fingers on the stick, keep your thumb on the side of the stick, keep the fulcrum secure, and watch your angle.

Sticking Exercise

Practice the following sticking patterns with the metronome set at 150, 170, and 190 **bpm** (beats per minute). When playing along with the audio, go through each line four times and then continue.

1. RRRR LLLL		13. LLLL RRRR	
2. RRLL RRLL		14. LLRR LLRR	
3. RLRL RLRL		15. LRLR LRLR	
4. RLRR LRLL		16. LRLL RLRR	
5. RLLR LRRL		17. LRRL RLLR	
6. RRLR LLRL		18. LLRL RRLR	
7. RLRL LRLR		19. LRLR RLRL	
8. RRRL RRRL		20. LLLR LLLR	
9. RLLL RLLL		21. LRRR LRRR	
10. RLRL RRLL		22. LRLR LLRR	
11. RLRL RRRL		23. LRLR LLLR	
12. RLRL RLLL		24. LRLR LRRR	

14

BASS DRUM TECHNIQUE

The bass drum is commonly referred to as the **kick drum**. It is struck with a bass drum pedal that is played with the foot. The bass drum beater is usually made of hard felt or wood. The spring tension should be set so the beater does not contact the head when the foot is resting on the pedal. The tighter the tension, the faster and stronger the rebound will be from the pedal. Heel down and heel up are the two basic methods for playing the kick:

Heel Down
This technique is usually for more low-end volume. The heel is down with the foot flat on the pedal. The foot returns immediately to the "up" position.

Heel Up
This technique is used for more high-end volume and can give more power. Simply lift the heel up and use just the ball of the foot to press the pedal. The foot returns immediately to the "up" position. This is useful for playing multiple strokes on the bass drum.

Open Tone
An **open tone** is created when the beater is allowed to rebound off the bass drumhead. This produces more of a resonant bass drum sound.

Closed Tone
A **closed tone** is created when the beater sticks (or is "buried") into the bass drumhead. This produces more of a punchy and dry bass drum sound.

Open and closed tone sounds are utilized by most drummers from time to time. The tuning of your drum and style of music you are playing may also help determine what type of sound is needed.

HI-HAT TECHNIQUE
(cont.)

The hi-hat, sometimes called the "sock cymbal," involves the same two techniques as the bass drum. The foot on the hi-hat pedal can be played heel down while you are using sticks on the hi-hat cymbal, or the drummer can use the heel-up technique for creating a "chick" or "splash" sound. You can make a crisper hi-hat sound with a harder push of the foot; the tighter the tension, the faster and stronger the rebound from the pedal.

The foot techniques below are used for more rhythmic playing with the hi-hat. Use the hi-hat clutch on the top cymbal to adjust the space between the cymbals. Generally, keep the cymbals about one inch apart.

Heel-Toe
This technique is used when playing on beats 2 and 4. The heel rises up as the ball of the foot presses the pedal; creates a rocking motion.

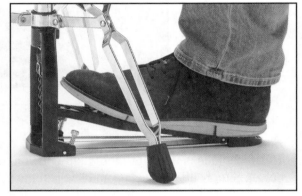

Toe
The ball of the foot bounces while keeping the leg raised; used when playing fast rhythms.

LESSON 2: MUSIC READING BASICS

QUICK TIP – Counting aloud is one of the best ways for a drummer to learn how to internalize tempo and rhythm. If you can't say it, you can't play it!

First, let's look at some basic musical terms:

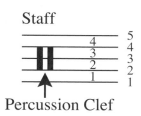

Staff

Percussion Clef

Staff – Made up of 5 lines and 4 spaces, counted from the bottom to the top

Percussion Clef – Denotes music of indefinite pitch

Bar Lines – Divide the staff into measures

Measures (or **bars**) **–** The space between bar lines

Double Bar Lines – Mark the end of a section

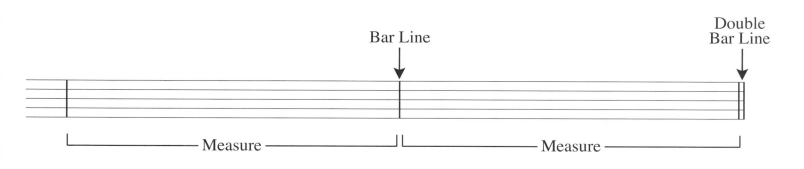

Repeat Signs – Repeat everything in between the dots

For drumset playing, each line and each space on the staff represents a different drum or cymbal. Using the staff below, see if you can find the different parts of the drumset.

Crash Cymbal	Hi-Hat	Open Hi-Hat	Closed Hi-Hat	Ride Cymbal	Ride Cymbal Bell

Mounted Tom High	Mounted Tom Low	Snare Drum	Snare Drum Cross-Stick	Floor Tom	Bass Drum	Hi-Hat with Foot

Time Signature – The stacked numbers located at the beginning of a piece of music. The top number indicates how many **beats** (counts) are in each measure. The bottom number indicates what type of note will get the beat. (Basic note values are detailed below.) A time signature is also commonly called a **meter**.

 The top number indicates how many beats are in each measure. In this case, there are 4 beats in each measure.
The bottom number indicates what type of note will get the beat. In this case, a quarter note equals 1 beat.

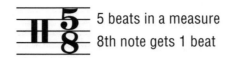 2 beats in a measure
quarter note gets 1 beat

5 beats in a measure
8th note gets 1 beat

 3 beats in a measure
16th note gets 1 beat

BASIC NOTE VALUES

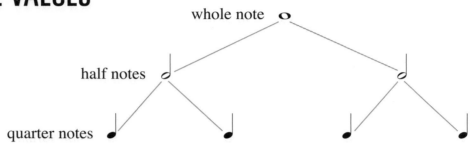

In 4/4 time:

- A **whole note** is 4 counts
- A **whole rest** is 4 counts of silence

- A **half note** is 2 counts
- A **half rest** is 2 counts of silence

- A **quarter note** is 1 count
- A **quarter rest** is 1 count of silence

Check Your Note Values

Try this short exercise to review the basic note values. Play the lines below using the snare drum in lines 1 and 3 and the bass drum in lines 2 and 4.

18

Combining Snare and Bass Drum

These exercises include quarter notes, half notes, and their matching rests.

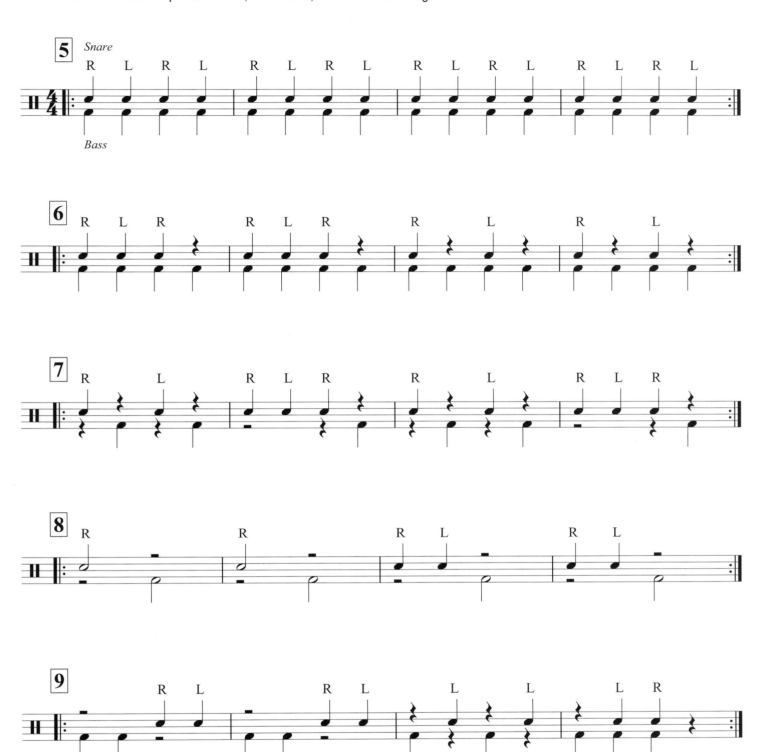

LESSON 3: COORDINATION

QUICK TIP – The sound of the ride cymbal is determined by the position of the cymbal, the grip on the stick, and the stroke. This is also true for the other instruments within the drumset.

Learning to ride a bike is a type of physical coordination that almost everyone can relate to. It takes time and repetition to ride the bike with such balance that you will not fall down, but rather, sail down the road. Playing drumset also requires physical coordination since all four limbs are used.

MOVING THE RIGHT HAND

A drummer's right hand will spend much time on the hi-hat and ride cymbal. The main function of the hi-hat and ride cymbal is that of "time-keeping." When playing with sticks on the hi-hat, the right stick will cross over the snare drum; keep the left foot pressed down on the hi-hat pedal so the cymbals stay closed.

Some drummers will use their left hand on the hi-hat to keep time as well. This "open-handed" style of drumming is very popular. Left-handed drummers sometimes prefer this because it feels natural to their dominant hand. Experiment with both options and choose whatever style fits you best.

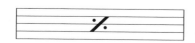

One-Measure Repeat Sign – Looks similar to the percentage symbol (%) and indicates to play the previous measure again. This symbol is used often in drumset music.

Coordination Exercise

Play the first two exercises using just the hi-hat and the snare drum. After you complete them, then insert the bass drum in place of the snare drum part, as seen in exercises 3 and 4.

Let's try putting it all together for our first rock beat!

THE RIDE CYMBAL

The largest cymbal on the drumset is called the ride cymbal because you "ride" on it with a steady pattern. The ride cymbal is a very important time keeper. The sound of the ride cymbal can be determined by three factors: how the cymbal is positioned, the grip, and the stroke.

Due to the tilt and angle of the ride cymbal, drummers will have to slightly turn their right hand outward for a more comfortable stroke on the cymbal. Playing with the thumb in the upward position is referred to as **French grip**. This also allows for easier use of fingers for faster tempos on the ride cymbal. The ride cymbal is usually played about a third of the way in from the outer edge. Try to keep the bead of the stick flat on the cymbal for a pure sound.

Playing on the **bell** (or dome) of the cymbal creates a bell-like sound:

Use the shoulder of the stick at the edge for a more crash-like sound:

Let's play our rock beat using the ride cymbal instead of the hi-hat.

> **Balance** – The volume of each instrument in the drumset should be balanced and consistent. Listen carefully to yourself to ensure that all sounds are blending.

When playing music that is longer than two or four bars, the drummer needs to keep track of how many measures they have played. Many times it will be based on a musical phrase but not always. The following examples show some different ways of counting and keeping track of where you are in the music.

  "BACK ON TRACK"
(cont.)

Try out your new rock beat with this song example.

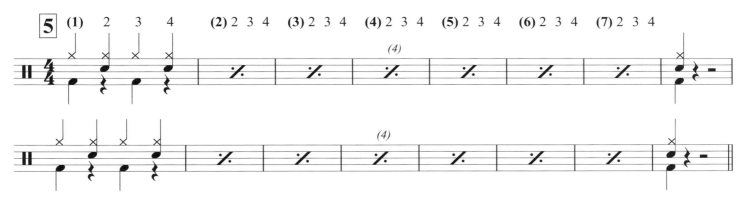

  "LET'S WALTZ"
(cont.)

This example is in 3/4 time (three beats per measure; quarter note equals one beat). Notice the shorthand for writing out numerous repeated measures.

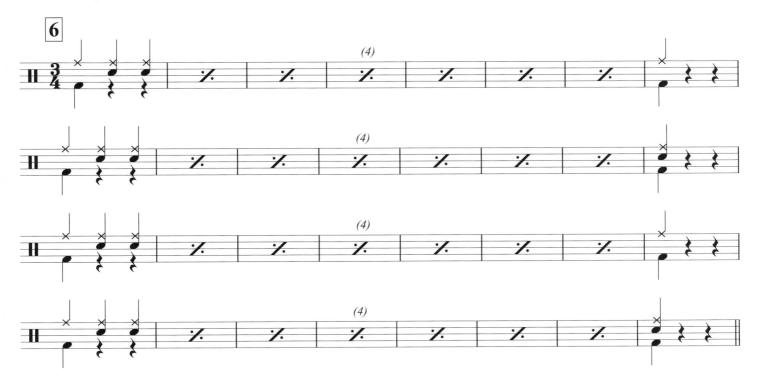

LESSON 4: 8TH NOTES

QUICK TIP – The foundation of a rock groove is based upon the relationship of the pattern between the snare drum and bass drum.

TECHNIQUE

Paradiddles – Rudiments are essential sticking patterns every drummer should know. **Paradiddle** rudiments are made up of a combination of single strokes followed by **double strokes** (two single strokes played by the same hand).

Single Paradiddle:	**R L R R L R L L**
Double Paradiddle:	**R L R L R R L R L R L L**
Triple Paradiddle:	**R L R L R L R R L R L R L R L L**
Paradiddle diddle:	1. **R L R R L L R L R R L L**
	2. **L R L L R R L R L L R R**

This lesson will add **8th notes** to our beats. An 8th note is easily identified because it looks like a quarter note, but with a single **flag** attached to the **stem**. Successive 8th notes can be joined together with a single **beam**. 8th notes divide the beat into two equal parts. So two 8th notes equal one quarter note.

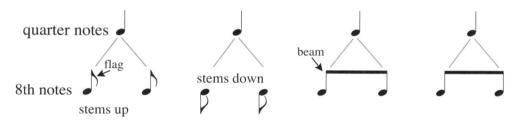

8th-Note Exercise

Play a few lines on the practice pad while using the metronome and counting aloud. Also try counting the 8th-note pulse to yourself while playing the exercise: "1 and 2 and 3 and 4 and." When counting, the numbers are considered the **downbeats** while the "ands" (&) are called **upbeats**.

Here is a paradiddle exercise using different combinations and various meter changes.

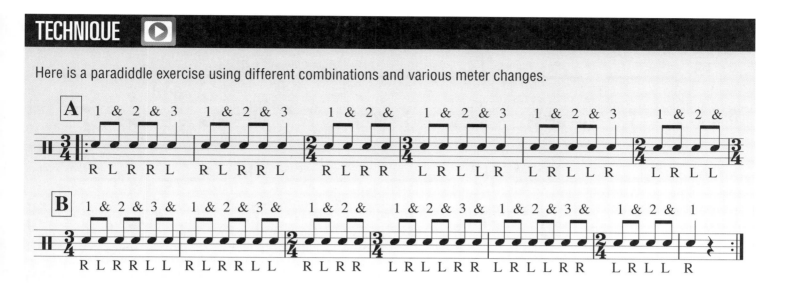

Steady 8th Note Limb Coordination

Try keeping a steady 8th-note pulse with your right hand while playing an independent rhythm with the left hand, and then your right foot.

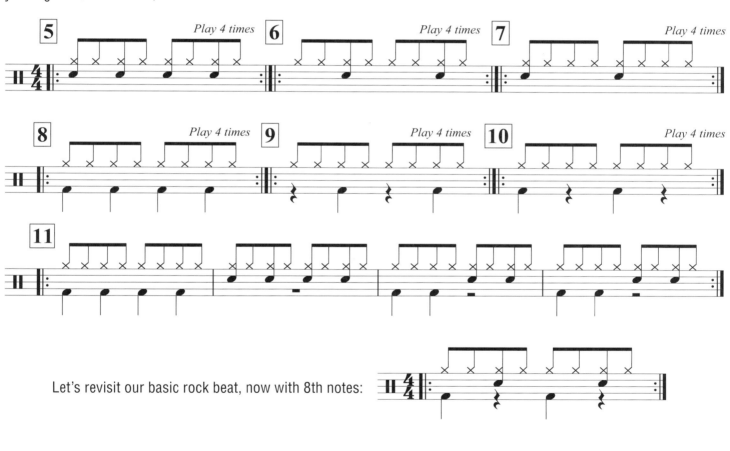

Let's revisit our basic rock beat, now with 8th notes:

"HOUSE BEAT"

More 8th-Note Beats

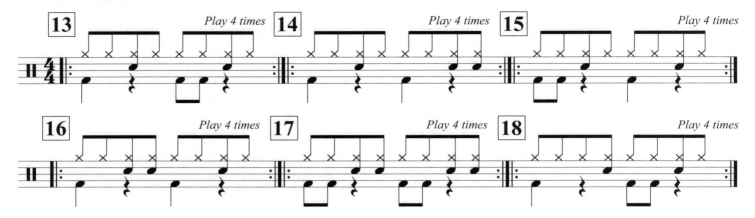

Extra Foot Work

For some extra practice, play these lines that include only the bass drum and hi-hat.

"8 BALL WILLIE"

LESSON 5: PLAYING THE TOMS

> **QUICK TIP –** Different musical styles require different dynamic considerations. Use your ears and a musical touch.

DYNAMICS

The degree of softness and loudness in which you play is determined by symbols known as **dynamics**. To achieve a difference in volume will require a change in stick heights.

pp	**pianissimo**	=	very soft
p	**piano**	=	soft
mp	**mezzo piano**	=	medium soft
mf	**mezzo forte**	=	medium loud
f	**forte**	=	loud
ff	**fortissimo**	=	very loud
sfz	**sforzando**	=	with sudden force or emphasis
$<$	**crescendo** (*cresc.*)		*to grow*; means a gradual increase in volume
$>$	**diminuendo** (*dim.*)		*to diminish*; means a gradual decrease in volume

Dynamic Exercise

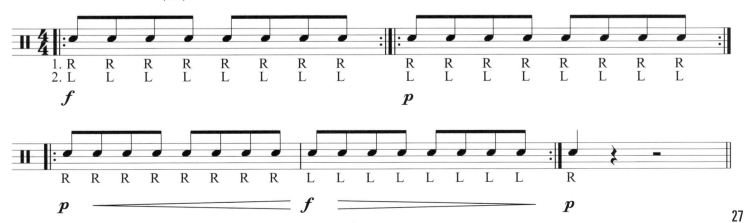

THE TOMS

Another important part of learning the drumset is becoming comfortable with moving around the toms. Let's try a few exercises that start with moving from the snare drum to the high tom, and then to the floor tom.

Toms Exercise

Exercises 5–8 include dynamic markings; be sure to play them!

Quarter-Note Beats

"EL GATO"

Play 3 times

Beats with Toms

Extra Foot Work

Attempt the previous exercises 1–8 with the hi-hat foot on beats 2 and 4, similar to the pattern below.

Two-Measure Repeat Sign – similar to the one-measure repeat, it means to repeat the previous two measures.

"JUNGLE BEAT JIM"

Rehearsal Marks – letters or numbers that are usually shown in a box or circle to indicate a different section of music, and most often a different groove.

"AIN'T NO GROOVE LIKE THE ONE I GOT"

In this song chart, you'll see rehearsal marks plus some other new symbols. The "band hits" (also called "ensemble hits") show slashes in the measure below; these tell you to continue playing the previous groove until the indicated 8th-note hit on the upbeat of beat 4. Listen to the demo track or watch the video to hear and understand how these function in the chart.

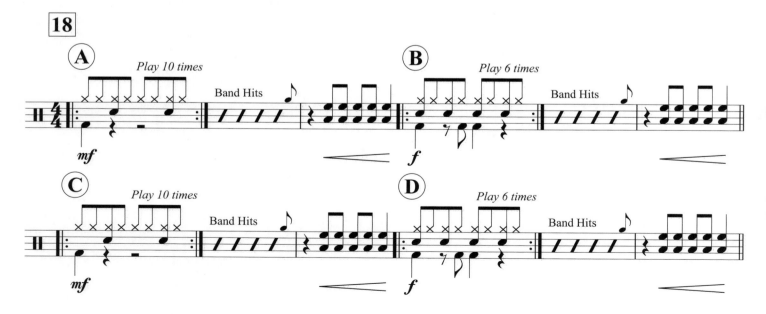

LESSON 6: TIES AND RESTS

QUICK TIP – The repetitive process known as building "muscle memory" is necessary in becoming a proficient drummer. Patterns, stickings, and coordination should become second nature.

UNDERSTANDING TIES AND RESTS

 A **tie** is a curved line connecting the heads of two or more notes, indicating that they are to be played as a single note. The duration of all the tied notes together is equal to the sum of the individual note values.

 In drumming, an easy way to think of a tie is to simply not play the following note. A tie is sometimes used to indicate "let vibrate" (or "let ring") when hitting a cymbal.

8th rests get the same value as the 8th notes. In other words, the 8th rest is a half beat of silence.

Ties and Rests Exercise

Remember, when two notes are joined by a tie, do not play the second note. Try the first four exercises below to get the idea. Then play the subsequent exercises that include quarter notes on the bass drum against different rhythms on the snare drum.

Basic Beats and Grooves

The following beats include 8th notes and rests, and 13–15 feature an upbeat 8th-note feel.

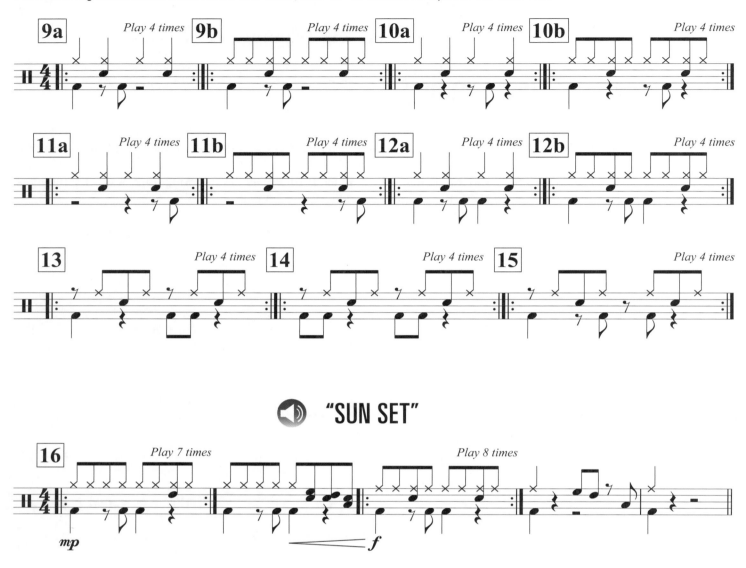

"SUN SET"

ACCENTS

An **accent** looks like this: > It means to play with more emphasis, relative to the marked dynamic level.

The crash cymbal is used to accent a musical moment, add more color, or to indicate the start or end of a musical section. It is most often struck with the shoulder of the stick on the outer edge of the cymbal. The crash cymbal is often notated with a tie indicating to let the cymbal vibrate.

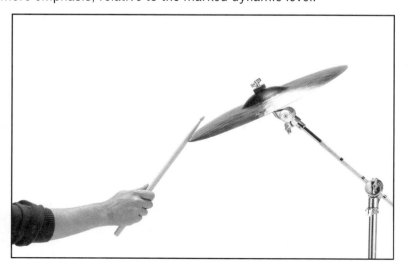

Beats with the Crash

Try a few quarter-note beats in 3/4 meter that include the crash cymbal.

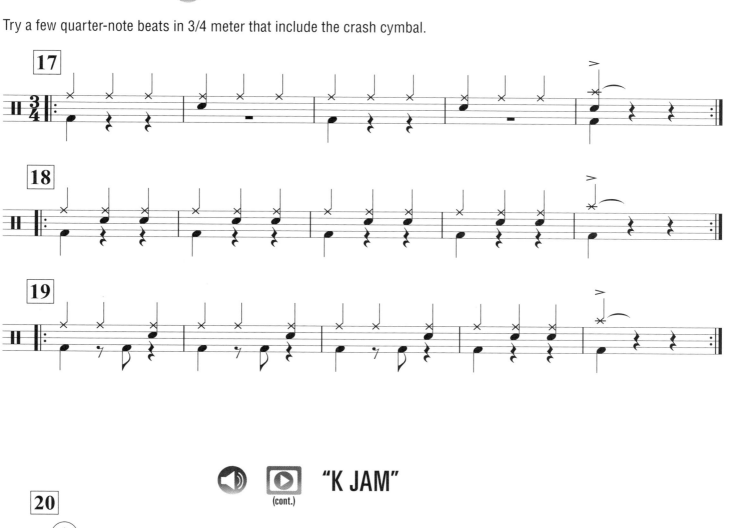

"K JAM" (cont.)

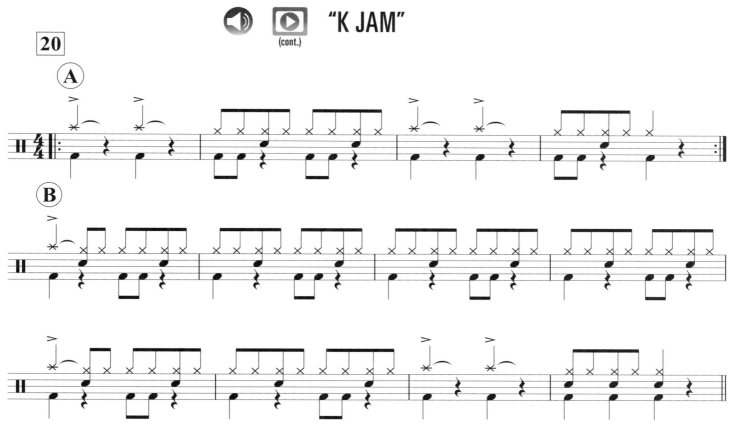

LESSON 7: NEW STROKES

CONTROLLING YOUR STROKES

Down Stroke – The **down stroke** (or **controlled stroke**) is basically a stroke that does not freely rebound by itself. After you strike the drum, try to freeze the stick about two to three inches from the top head.

Avoid squeezing the stick too tight as it may shake or buzz on the head. Try a slightly firmer squeeze at the fulcrum (index finger and thumb) and then immediately release upon impact. The timing has to be correct for this method to work.

Up Stroke – Check out Example A below. Notice there is a note in between the accented down strokes. Play them by simply "dropping" the stick as you turn your wrist for the next accent. This is referred to as an **up stroke**. Think of lifting with the back of the stick first.

Tap Stroke – Now look at Example B. Notice there are two notes between the accented down strokes. Up strokes are not used repetitively, but rather, they are used prior to an accent. The first unaccented note in Example B should be played as a **tap stroke**. Use a very small amount of wrist for these strokes. Play the tap strokes two to three inches above the drumhead.

DOTTED NOTES

A **dot** behind a note increases its length by adding half of its original value. For instance, a **dotted half note** is equal to three counts. A **dotted quarter note** is equal to one and a half counts. Check out the following exercises.

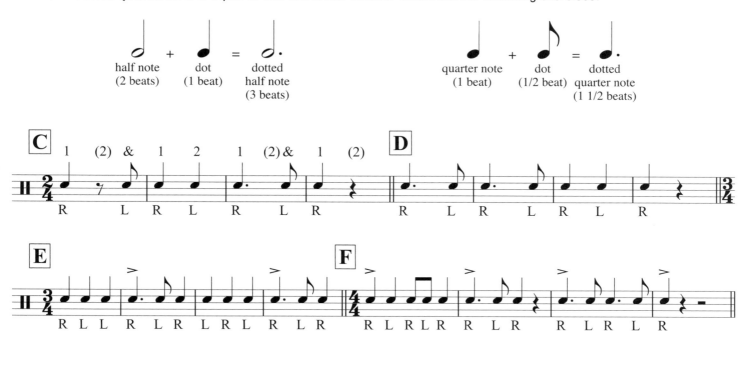

Dotted Quarter Note Grooves

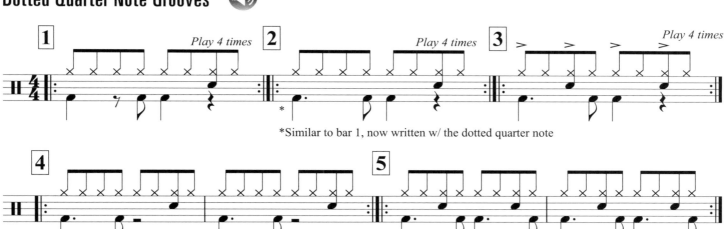

*Similar to bar 1, now written w/ the dotted quarter note

Sometimes when a musical phrase is repeated, there may be two (or more) different endings. This is indicated in written music with **first and second endings**. In the following song, play through the first ending, then repeat. The second time through, skip over the first ending and proceed to the second ending.

"SECOND AVENUE"

CROSS-STICK

Cross-stick is a technique that drummers use to create a sound like that of a wood block. Place the butt end of the stick about three to four inches over the snare drum rim while the palm of the left hand rests near the center of the drumhead. Lift the butt end of the stick to strike the rim while the palm rests on the drumhead. Cross-stick is commonly used in ballads, Latin music, and much more.

Cross-Stick Exercise
(cont.)

> **Fermata** – a symbol placed over or under a note or rest indicating to hold or sustain it beyond the written value, at the discretion of the performer(s).

"BALLAD"

This song features several drum **fills**, a concept explored further in the next lesson.

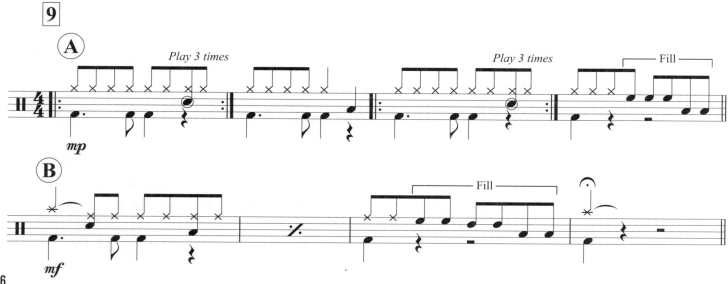

LESSON 8: DRUM FILLS

QUICK TIP – Learning how to practice is one of most important steps in becoming a successful drummer. Go slowly, use a metronome, count aloud, and stay relaxed.

TECHNIQUE

Hand-to-Hand Accents

Start by alternating some tap strokes with a right-hand accent:

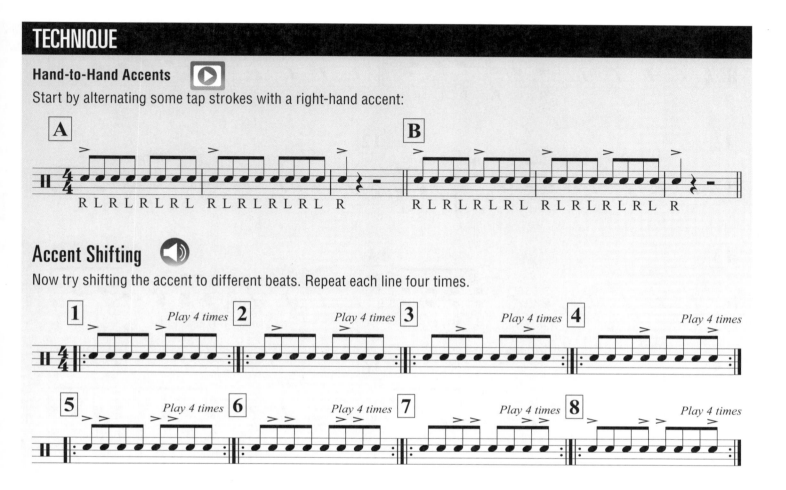

Accent Shifting

Now try shifting the accent to different beats. Repeat each line four times.

FILLS

A **drum fill** is a short break in the groove that usually indicates the end of a phrase or the start of something new. The fill serves as a bridge to "fill in the gap" between musical sections. Selecting what to play and what to play it on is the drummer's choice.

Here is an example of a groove with a fill taking place on the last two counts of the last measure. Searching for ideas can be the most challenging thing for young drummers. Use basic rhythms you have learned so far and try moving them around the drums. For this example, plug the fills C–F into the groove pattern below:

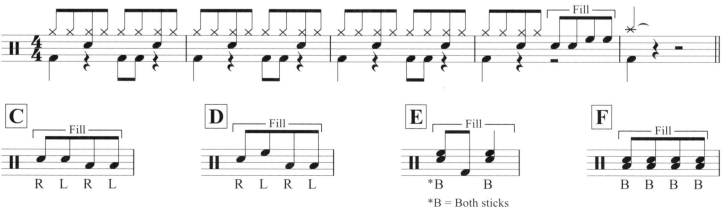

37

TIME-KEEPING

Remember to practice fills with a sense of "time-keeping." Try playing three bars of time followed by a one-bar fill. **Time** refers to playing a groove or pattern continuously, or "keeping time." In written music, **slash notation** is used to signal time. Drummers should develop an inner sense of time, like an imaginary metronome.

Fills Exercise

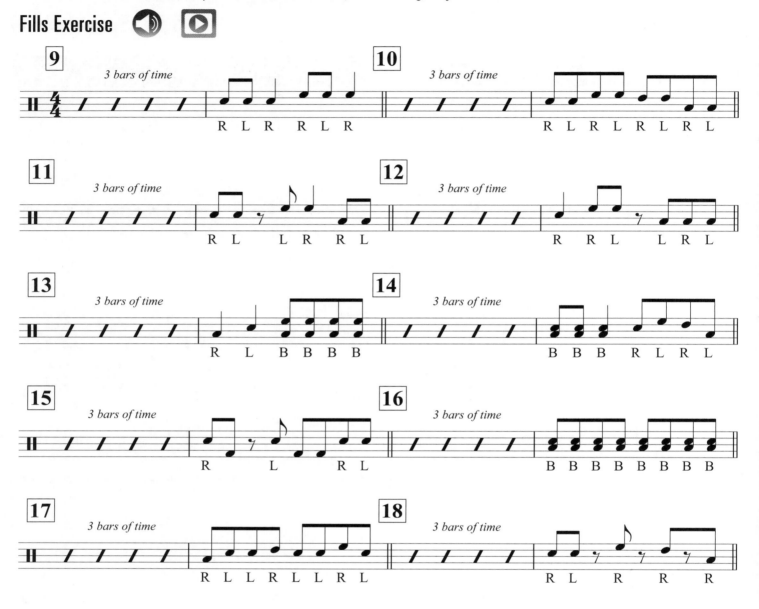

Country Two-Beat Feel

Another common groove is the country two-beat feel. Check it out:

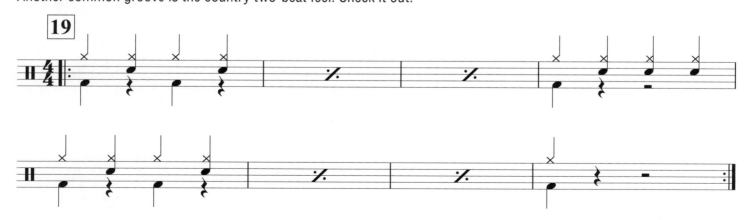

OPEN HI-HAT

Opening the hi-hat is another color you can add to your drumset playing. Occasionally opening the hi-hat can create additional energy and contrast. Just raise your foot off the pedal as you strike the hi-hat and then close the cymbals by pressing the foot pedal back down as you strike the hi-hat again (usually with the shoulder of the stick). Try this little exercise:

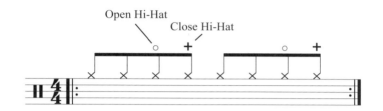

"DOWNTOWN DISCO"

LESSON 9: MORE GROOVES AND FILLS

QUICK TIP – Remember that drum fills can serve as a bridge leading from one phrase to another. Try starting drum fills softer and crescendo into the next phrase to make it musical.

TECHNIQUE

Flams – The **flam** is made up of two notes: as seen in the example below, the primary note (regular-sized note) and the **grace note** (the small note) that precedes it. These notes do not strike the drum at the same time, but they are very close. The grace note is struck from two to three inches above the drum, while the primary note is about nine inches above. Think of the flam as a thicker single stroke, though not necessarily heavier.

Two-Bar Beat Patterns

All of the beat patterns we have learned thus far have been one-bar beat patterns. However, two-bar beat patterns are just as common and can add more interest to a groove.

Two-Bar Fill Ideas

Now try some two-bar fill ideas. Remember that slashes mean to keep time; play a beat you are comfortable with during those measures, or play the beat you hear on the demonstration audio track.

Shifting the Backbeat

The snare drum **backbeat**, which is usually considered the emphasis of beats 2 and 4, can be shifted to other beats to create various types of grooves with a different feel, as in lines 11–14 of the following exercise. And moving the snare drum to upbeats can create even more types of interesting groove patterns with rhythmic interest, as in lines 15–17.

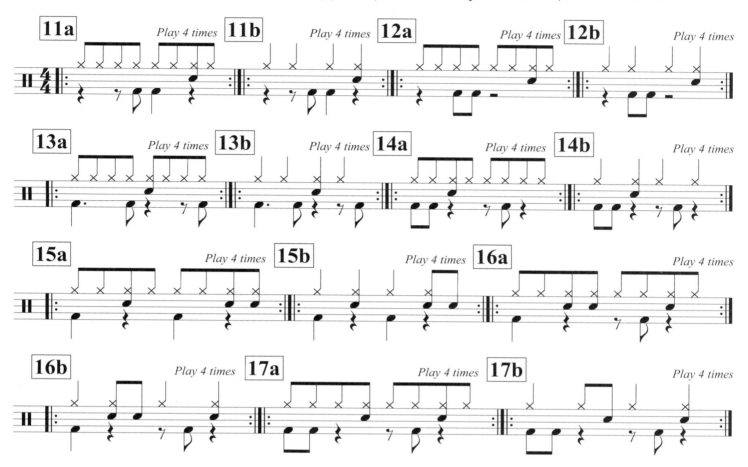

"MOVE OVER MOTOWN"

For the C and D sections, you'll see slash notation used to denote playing time.

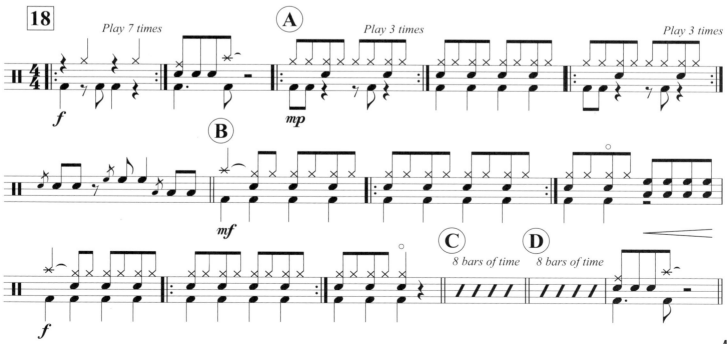

LESSON 10: MUSICAL FORM

QUICK TIP – Most often a drum groove in a song's chorus may slightly change from the one used in the verse. This type of variation can include changing from hi-hat to ride cymbal, or going from an 8th-note groove to a quarter-note groove.

Phrasing Exercise 1

Most songs are divided into sections such as the intro, verse, chorus, bridge, solo section, and ending. Each of these sections includes phrases. Just like sentences make up a paragraph, musical phrases make up a section of music. The most common length of a phrase is four or eight bars. Play along with the following tracks and notice that the crash cymbal marks the start of each phrase.

Phrasing Exercise 2

Intro – occurs at the start of a tune and "introduces" the song.

Verse – one of the main sections. Usually there will be more than one, but the music will remain the same while the lyrics change.

Chorus – another main section that contains the "hook" of the song. There might be several chorus sections in a song, but the music *and* lyrics will be the same.

Bridge – serves as a transition from one section to another. The harmonic structure may be slightly altered here.

Solo Section – might be added to a song as another type of transition. Solos usually occur over the verse or chorus structure.

Ending (or outro) – the section that brings the song to an end. This could be done as a fade out or with a small tag to bring the tune to a stop.

SONG FORM BREAKDOWN

In the following examples, notice the small changes in the musical form of the same tune.

Paradise – Version 1

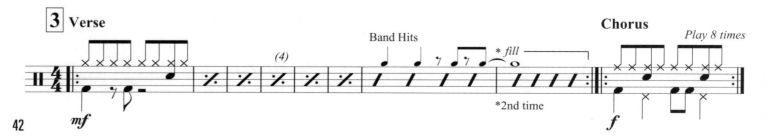

Paradise – Version 2 🔊

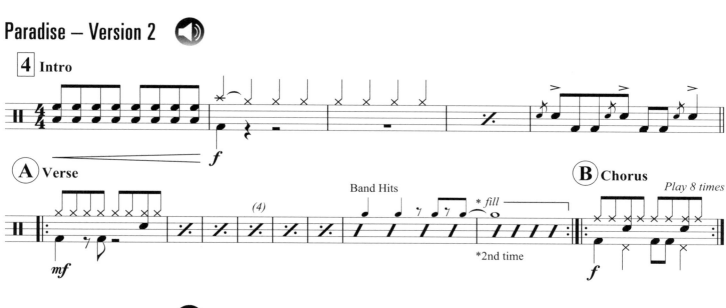

Paradise – Version 3 🔊

🔊 ▶️ **"PARADISE" (Full Version)**

You may notice a few subtle additions to the drum part on the accompanying audio demonstration. Adding your own ideas is something you can experiment with as well—a fun and productive way to develop your personal drumming style.

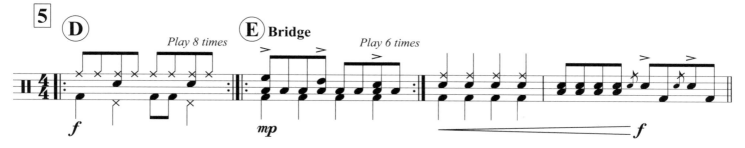

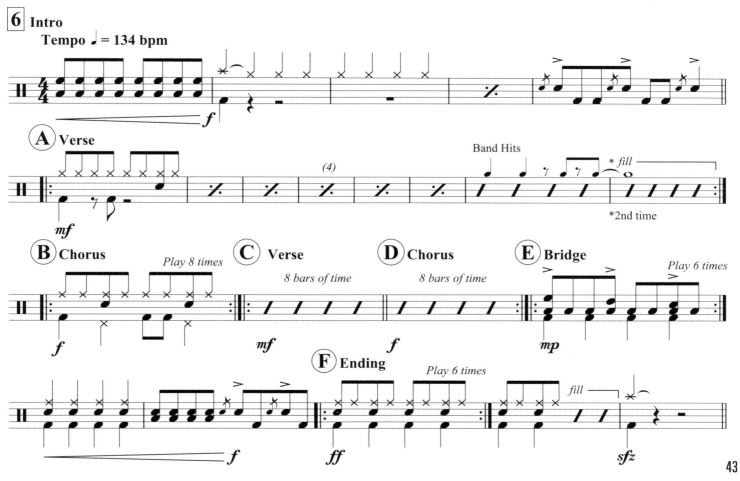

LESSON 11: 16TH NOTES

QUICK TIP – Subdividing music is the process of breaking down a rhythm into smaller parts so that it may be played with greater accuracy.

 16th notes have two flags or a double beam. These notes are twice as fast as 8th notes. This means that two 16th notes equal one 8th note. Therefore, four 16ths equal one quarter note. New syllables will be needed to count this aloud: "1-e-&-ah, 2-e-&-ah," etc. Check out the following examples.

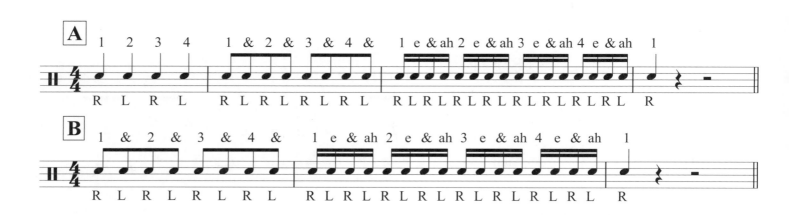

TECHNIQUE

Single Strokes – Single strokes are the basic foundation of technique for any drummer. Here are a few exercises that go from 8th to 16th single strokes. Remember to stay relaxed and let the stick rebound; avoid gripping the sticks too tightly.

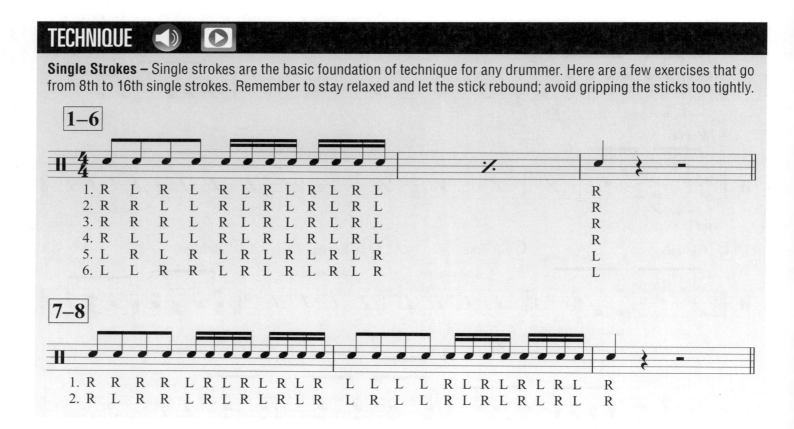

16TH-NOTE GROOVES

Using 16th notes in a groove pattern is another fundamental requirement for a proficient drummer. Here are the three basic options:

C Use right hand only on the hi-hat:

D Use **alternate sticking** (RLRL, etc.) on the hi-hat:

E Use right hand only on the ride cymbal:

16th-Note Groove Exercise

Lines 9–13 below feature some 16th-note grooves and their optional ride patterns. The left column (9A–13A) should be played with alternate sticking on the hi-hat. The right column (9B–13B) should be played with the right hand on either the hi-hat or the ride cymbal. The snare and bass drum parts remain the same.

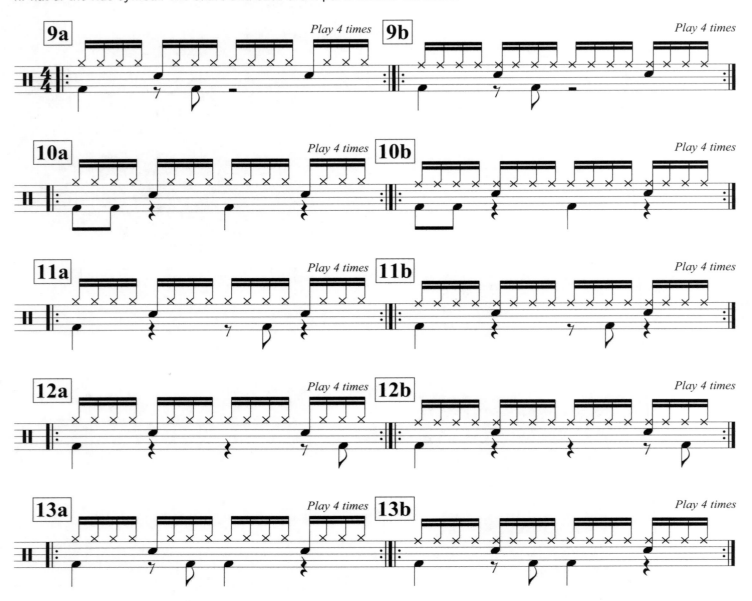

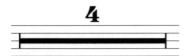

Multi-Measure Rest – this type of rest can be indicated as follows:

It means to rest the number of measures indicated by the number. In this example, rest for four measures. If there are four beats in a measure, it would be counted as:

(1) 2 3 4   (2) 2 3 4   (3) 2 3 4   (4) 2 3 4

If there are three beats in a measure:

(1) 2 3   (2) 2 3   (3) 2 3   (4) 2 3

The use of 16th notes in the right hand only works well for a rock ballad-type song. This groove is usually slower, allowing the right-hand 16th notes to flow very nicely within the time. In the third system, notice that the crash cymbal is hit on beat 1, then the measure is repeated. Typically, in drum charts, it is assumed that the crash is *not* hit again in the subsequent repeated measures.

"ROCK BALLAD #1"

"MADE IN THE USA"

LESSON 12: NEW RHYTHMS

QUICK TIP – When playing more rhythmic grooves with the bass drum, the "heel-up" technique can be very helpful. Some drummers utilize a "slide" stroke for quick passages with the foot.

New rhythms can be created by removing two 16th notes from a four-note group and replacing them with an 8th note. Here are the two most common:

New Rhythm Exercise 1

Practice the new rhythms in the following exercises. Note that New Rhythm Exercise 1 and 2 are combined as one continuous example on the accompanying audio tracks.

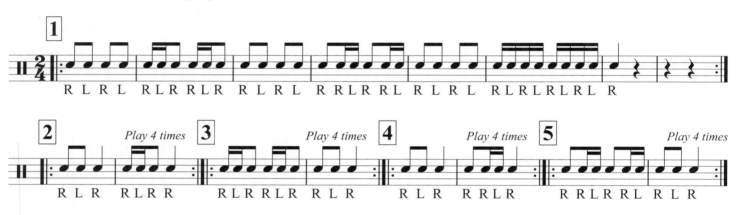

If the 8th note is removed and replaced with an 8th rest, the following two new rhythms are created:

New Rhythm Exercise 2
(cont.)

New Rhythm Grooves 1

Apply these new rhythms to the drumset by using the right hand for the hi-hat and the left hand for the snare drum. Note that New Rhythm Grooves 1 and 2 are combined as one continuous example on the accompanying audio tracks.

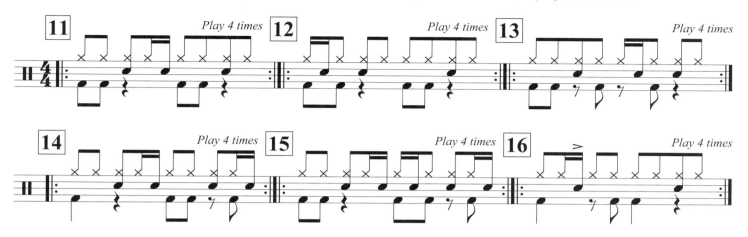

New Rhythm Grooves 2
(cont.)

Add the bass drum with these new rhythms. The following lines combine the bass drum with the same voice as the snare and hi-hat/ride. Lines 19–21 might need a little more bass drum practice.

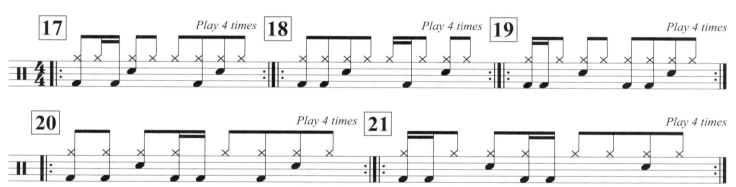

 "JOVIAL JUNIPER"

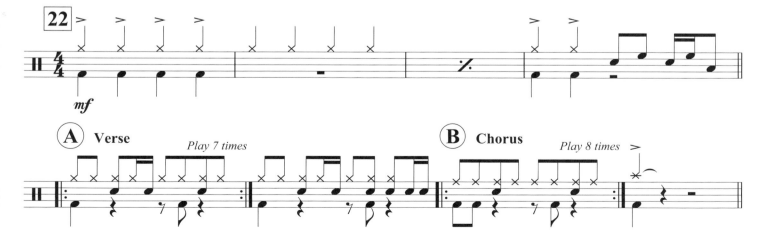

LESSON 13: 16TH-NOTE FILLS

QUICK TIP – Developing smooth 16th notes around the drumset can be achieved by practicing a continuous flow of them on every instrument of the set while using a metronome. Start slowly and gradually increase the tempo.

16ths Around the Drums

Developing a smooth flow of 16th notes around the drums is very crucial. Start with the following exercises:

One-Bar 16ths Fills

Try a few one-bar fill ideas using 16th notes:

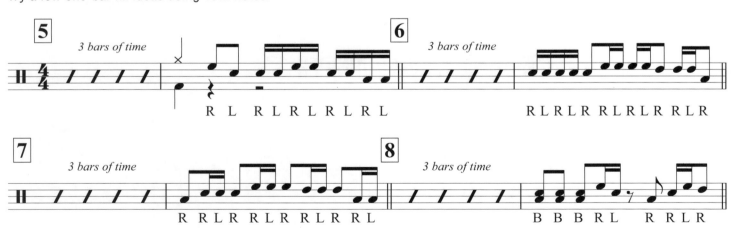

One- and Two-Beat 16ths Fills

16th notes are commonly used for a one- or two-beat fill at the end of a groove. Plug fills A–F into the groove patterns below.

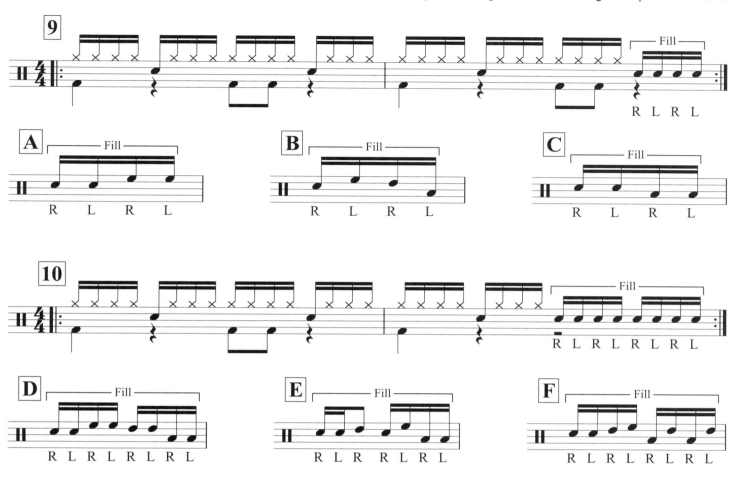

"RED 80"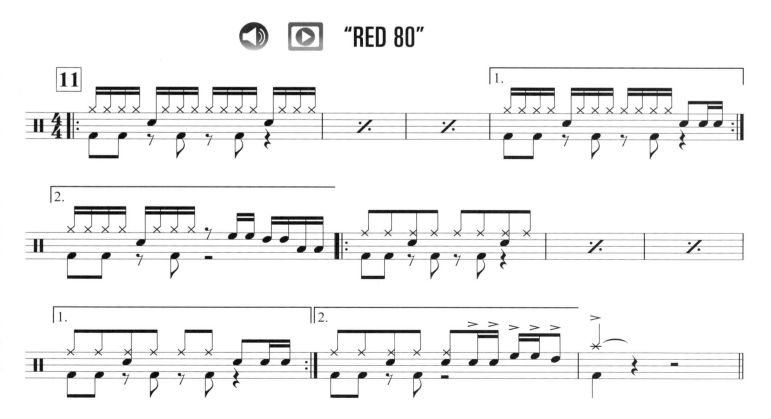

LESSON 14: TRIPLETS

QUICK TIP – In jazz playing, the term "comp" means to compliment ideas with your swinging ride cymbal.

UNDERSTANDING TRIPLETS

Until this lesson, all of our rhythms have been duple-based (evenly divided). It is now time to introduce a triple-based rhythm. The beat is divided equally into thirds, which we call **triplets**. Since there is no note value between an 8th and 16th note, triplets are notated as three 8th notes beamed together with a "3" marked above the group. This is called an **8th-note triplet**.

Notice the shift of sticking from the right to left hand when you play two counts of triplets.

Try the next exercise to get a feel for the different subdivisions you've learned thus far, including the new triplet. Remember to use a metronome for accuracy.

Triplet Exercise 1

Get acquainted with triplets in the following exercises 1–16. Note that Triplet Exercises 1 and 2 and the subsequent Triplet Stickings Exercise are combined as one continuous example on the accompanying audio tracks.

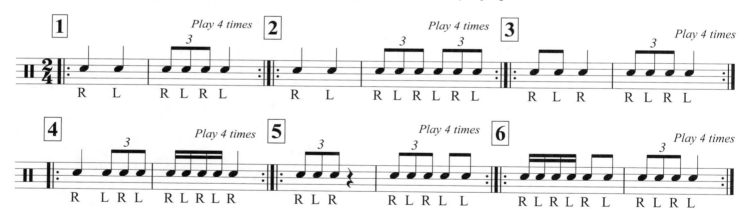

Triplet Exercise 2
(cont.)

The **quarter-note triplet** is also a common type of triplet rhythm that is created over two beats. If you alternate two 8th-note triplets, notice that the right hand by itself plays the quarter-note triplet rhythm.

Triplet Stickings Exercise
(cont.)

Triplet stickings are important in getting the "feel" of the triplet. Try some of these sticking patterns as triplets. Work on getting them to flow evenly while staying very relaxed. When practicing these with the audio, play each pattern four times, stopping on beat 2 of the fourth time, then proceed.

9. R L R L R L

10. L R L R L R

11. R R L R R L

12. L R R L R R

13. R L L R L L

14. R L R R L L

15. L R L L R R

16. R L L R L R

BASIC JAZZ BEAT
(cont.)

Jazz (swing) music is heavily influenced by triplet rhythms. As 8th-note and 16th-note repetitive grooves are to rock music, triplets are to jazz music. The triplet feel has to be as comfortable to the drumset player as any other repeating pattern. Here is the basic jazz ride pattern played on the ride cymbal. At slow and medium tempos it has the triplet feel, but at fast tempos it flattens out to straighter 8th notes.

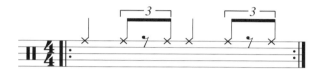

It is very common to see the basic jazz ride pattern written as a dotted 8th and 16th note, but it should still be played with a triplet feel.

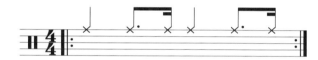

The hi-hat plays on beats 2 and 4 with the "rocking" or "heel-toe" technique. A crisp hi-hat "chick" on 2 and 4 is an important element of the jazz pattern.

It is not uncommon for the bass drum to maintain a very light "four on the floor" (one hit for each beat) during the ride patterns. It is almost not even heard, but kind of "feathered." The heel-down technique with a light open tone works best. However, the bass drum should mostly be used for accents and embellishing phrases.

Jazz Ride Exercise

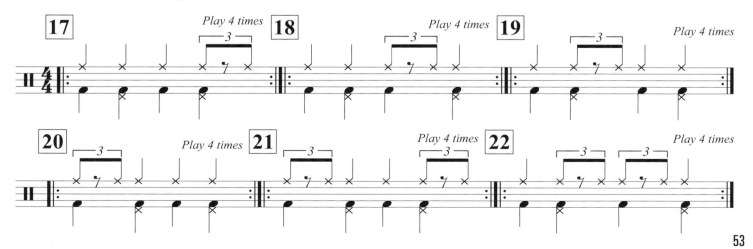

Comping Exercise

Once you have the ride cymbal pattern and hi-hat locked in, gradually add some "comping" rhythms on the snare drum. "Comp" means to accompany in a complimentary fashion. Notice that these rhythms all fit into the triplet feel.

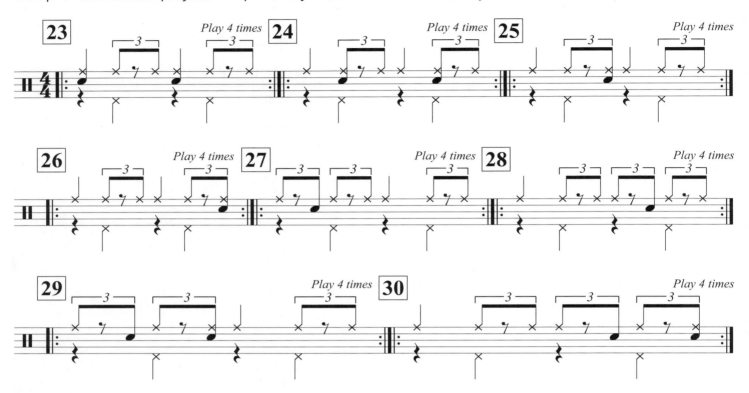

  "SWINGING FOR HAL"

(cont.)

Try adding some comp rhythms as you play through this tune.

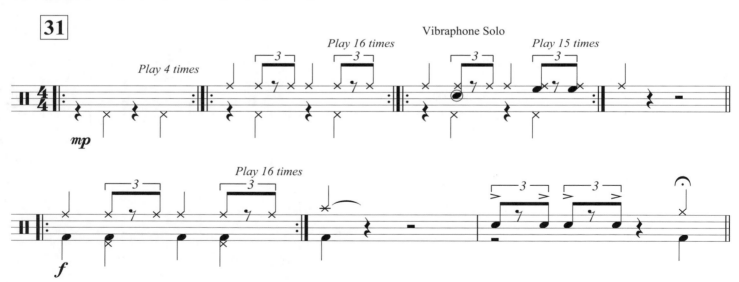

LESSON 15: JAZZ DRUMMING

QUICK TIP – The first step in jazz drumming is to develop some basic independence with triplet figures. This will help the novice drummer interact in jazz music.

TECHNIQUE

Shifting Accents with Triplets

Practicing shifting accents with different triplet stickings will provide a great opportunity to develop an even more fluid triplet feel.

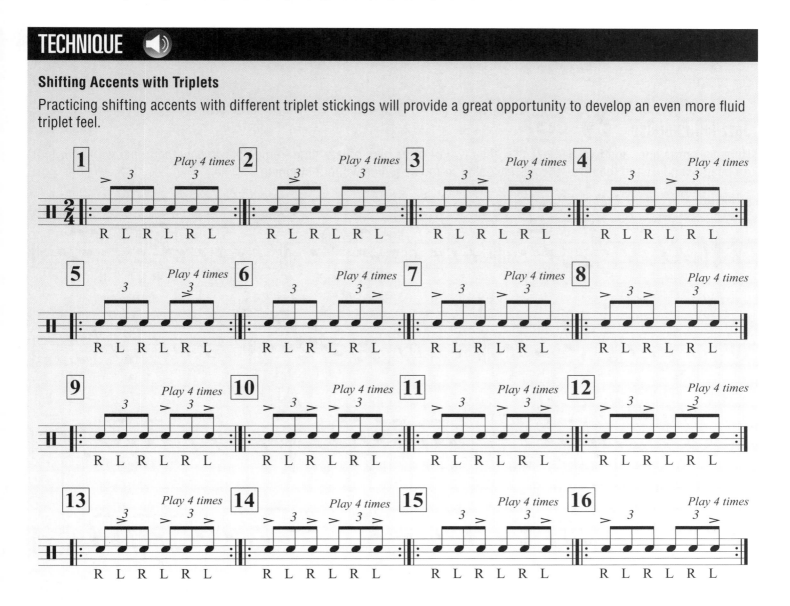

SWING FEEL

In jazz playing, written rhythms are meant to be played with a triplet feel, or **swing feel**. Even though you may see 8th notes in the notation, they should be played with a triplet feel. Many times, a triplet or swing indication (seen here; or simply the words "Swing Feel") will be given at the start of a piece of music telling the player to swing the 8th notes throughout.

The triplet graph below shows how the written 8th-note rhythms are swung.

JAZZ FILLS

As you learned in earlier lessons, drum fills can serve as a bridge to connect musical phrases. When playing jazz fills, the drummer will use a triplet feel rather than a duple feel. However, the notation is usually written with straight 8th notes, as mentioned earlier. Refer to the triplet graph to review this concept. Here is another example.

Jazz Fill Exercise

Here are some one- and two-bar jazz fills. Play two or three bars of jazz time (remember to play the hi-hat with your foot on beats 2 and 4) and then play the fill. Try going from line to line without stopping.

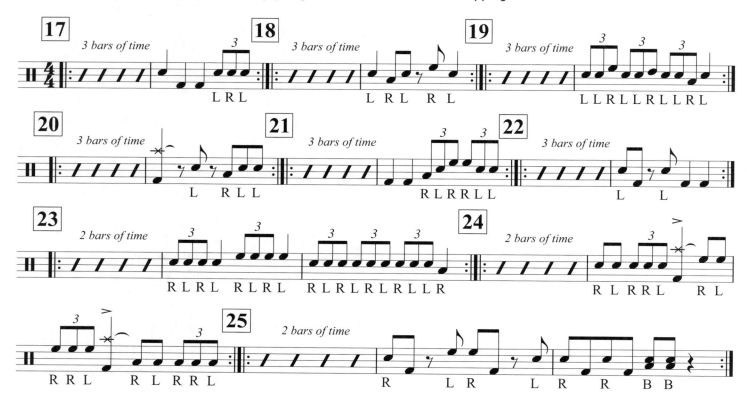

"BANANA BLUES"

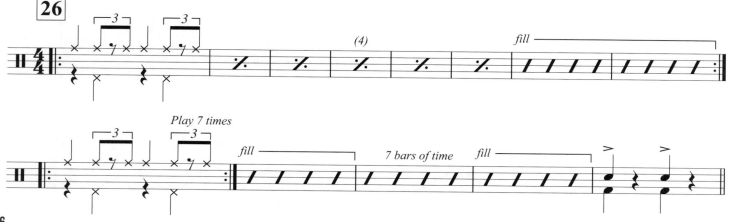

LESSON 16: THE SHUFFLE

> **QUICK TIP –** Early rock 'n' roll was the basis for many forthcoming styles of popular music.
> Shuffle beats can be heard in a lot of early rock 'n' roll music.

A very popular triplet-based rhythm is called the **shuffle**.
It consists of the first and third note of each triplet.

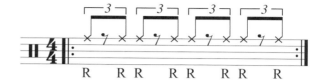

Basic Shuffles

Shuffles can be heard in all types of musical styles, such as blues, rock, country, and jazz. Here are a few basic shuffle variations:

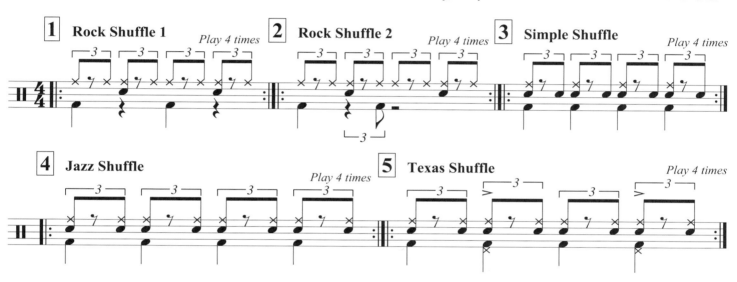

12-BAR BLUES

Drummers should be able to recognize a **12-bar blues** when they hear one. This is an extremely common repeating form where the chords change in bars 5, 7, 9, 10, and 11. Sometimes Roman numerals are used to represent the chords instead of letters. Use any of the above shuffles to play along with the next example and play close attention to the chord changes.

"BILLY'S BLUES"

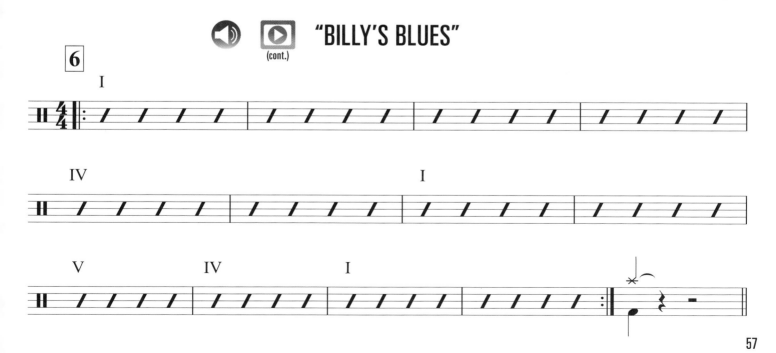

Sometimes drummers will use the hi-hat to play the ride cymbal pattern. Opening the hi-hat on beats 1 and 3 gives the groove a "two-beat feel." The hi-hat can be played alone or the bass drum can be added softly if there is a bass line in the actual music. Cross-stick can also be added for variety.

Hi-Hat Shuffle

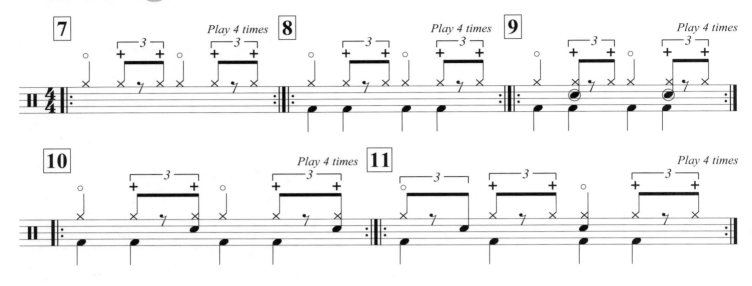

"TAKE THE TRAIN"

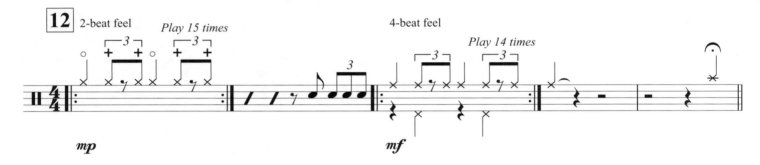

JAZZ WALTZ

The jazz **waltz** (in 3/4 meter) is most commonly played in a "one-beat feel" or a "three-beat feel." For a one-beat feel, the bass drum and snare drum are more active in the time while the ride cymbal and hi-hat are more subtle. In the three-beat feel, the ride cymbal and hi-hat are more focused while the bass drum and snare drum are more in the background. The bass player can also be very helpful in creating both of these feels.

Jazz Waltz Exercise

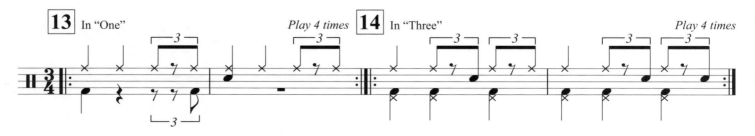

Jazz Waltz Variations

It is very common to hear different ride patterns in a 3/4 jazz waltz. Mix and match the variations shown below as you feel comfortable. The audio demonstration features an improvised mixture of all these different variations.

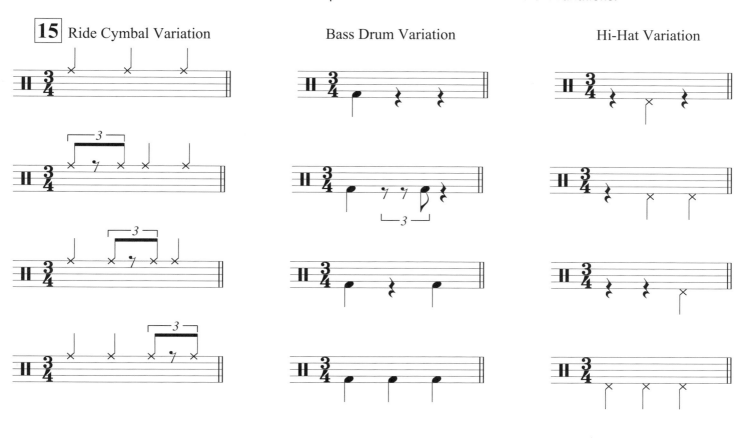

15 Ride Cymbal Variation   Bass Drum Variation   Hi-Hat Variation

"WALTZ FOR MADDY"

16

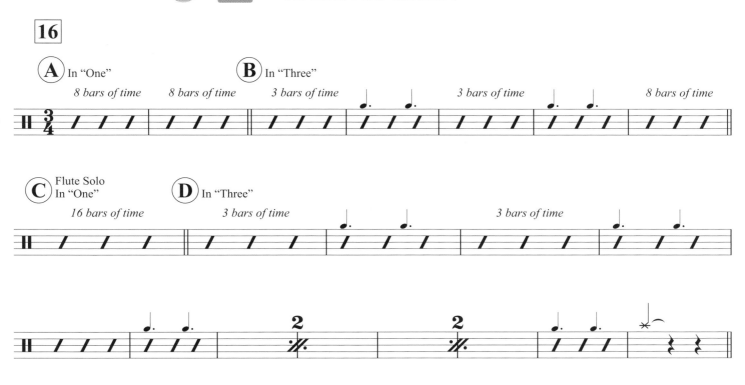

(A) In "One"   (B) In "Three"

8 bars of time   8 bars of time   3 bars of time   3 bars of time   8 bars of time

(C) Flute Solo In "One"   (D) In "Three"

16 bars of time   3 bars of time   3 bars of time

LESSON 17: NEW METERS

QUICK TIP – "Trading fours" is when a drummer alternates playing time for four measures and then plays a solo for four measures.

12/8 AND 6/8

Until this lesson, all of the time signatures have been in some type of duple meter. Changing the bottom number of a time signature to an "8" will result in a triple meter. In "8 time," the 8th note gets one beat. You can count the number of beats per measure (Example A) or count the division of three (Example B). B tends to be quite easier and lends itself to more of a "triplet feel."

12/8 and 6/8 Grooves

12/8 time can basically be read as 4/4 time, but the pulse is given to the dotted quarter note. This means there will be three 8th notes per beat instead of two. Some of the most popular early rock and blues music used the 12/8 groove. 6/8 time is another similar meter that can be heard in all types of music. Check out examples of both:

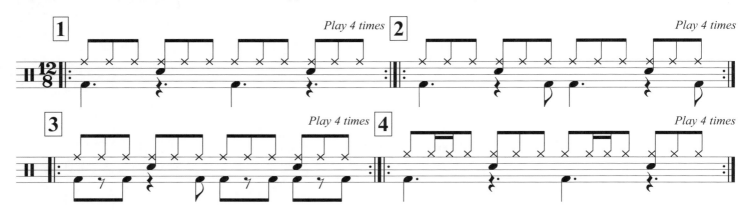

CUT TIME

 Another popular time signature is **cut time** (often represented by the symbol seen here). It is read with the half note, rather than the quarter note, getting the beat. In other words, it is 2/2 (instead of 4/4), which will ultimately create a "two feel." This time signature is often used for faster tempos because it is easier to read.

In cut time, the note values you know from 4/4 meter are cut in half:

- A whole note gets 2 counts
- A half note gets 1 count

- A quarter note gets a half count
- An 8th note gets a quarter count

Cut Time Beats

On the audio demonstration, each numbered example is played twice through, including the repeats.

ENCORE #1

Congratulations for making it through Book 1 of the *Hal Leonard Drumset Method*! Remember to download the extra content that comes with this book, which includes bonus practice material such as accent combinations and reading exercises. Here are two full song charts for study and practice. Be sure to continue your studies with Book 2!

ENCORE #2

This song chart includes new routing directions. **D.S. al Coda** means to repeat back to the sign (𝄋) and continue playing until the direction **To Coda**. At this point, you jump to the section marked "Coda" at the end to finish out the tune.

LESSON 18: LIMB INDEPENDENCE

QUICK TIP – When practicing different ostinato patterns, try to be aware of the notes that land within the 8th-note pulse. A solid groove depends on the consistent placement of these notes.

A common way to take a simple beat and transform it into another variation is by changing the ostinato pattern in the right hand. An **ostinato** pattern is a musical figure that is repetitive. For instance, the right hand usually plays 8th or 16th notes on the hi-hat or ride cymbal. Here is an example of taking a basic groove and changing the ostinato pattern. Keep in mind that these are just a few variations. Use your creativity to come up with patterns you like.

Ostinato Exercise

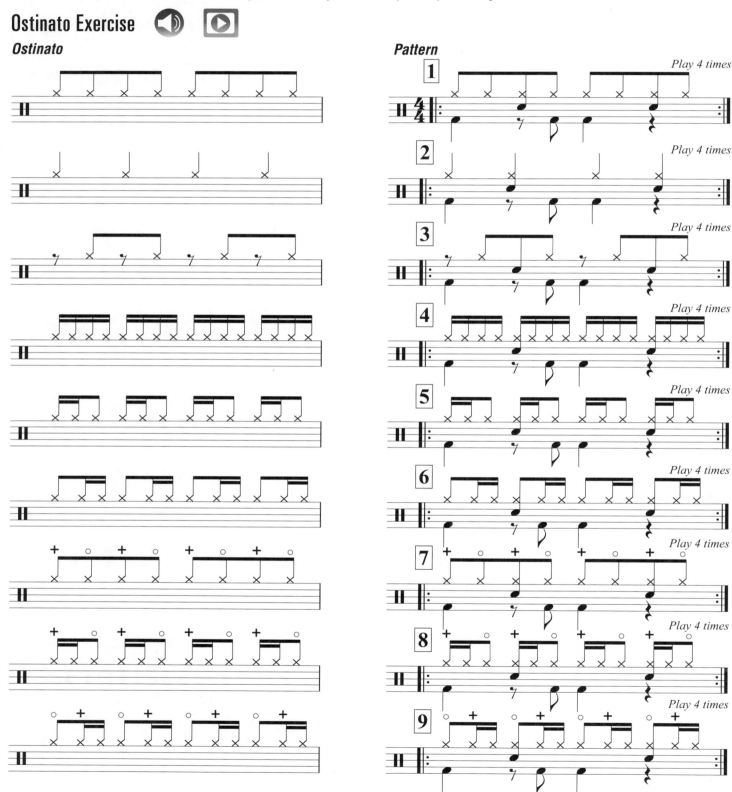

After you have mastered all of these different ostinato patterns with the right hand, try reversing the hands. Play the hi-hat ostinato with the left hand and the snare drum with the right hand. Take your time and practice slowly.

Independence Exercise

Four-limb independence can be practiced by adding left foot (stepping) hi-hat rhythms to the ostinato patterns. Play the following beats with the previous ostinato patterns, this time adding the left-foot ostinato patterns shown below (A–D) on the hi-hat. **Note:** on the audio demonstration track, only the A and C left-foot ostinato patterns are played.

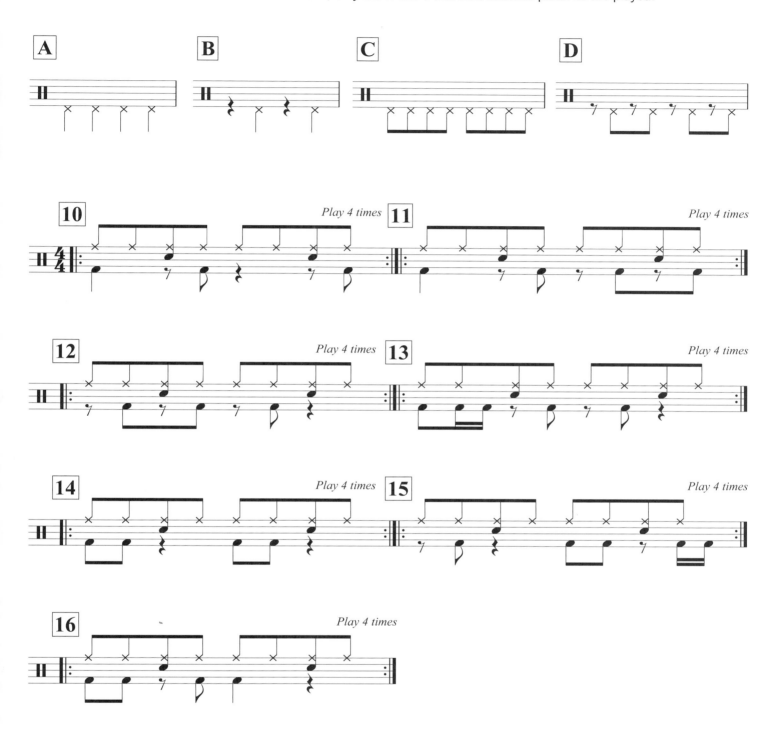

LESSON 19: HALF-TIME GROOVES

QUICK TIP – Be careful to visualize the music on the chart when playing in half-time. Since the backbeat occurs only on beat 3, the music tends to flow a bit faster from measure to measure.

Half-time feel is another type of groove that every drummer should know well. This occurs when the usual backbeat on beats 2 and 4 shifts to beat 3 instead. It gives the music a totally different feel even though the tempo has not changed. Many drummers tend to rush the tempo when playing half-time because there is more space between the backbeats. It is very important to hear all of the subdivisions in your head. Let's try a few half-time grooves:

Half-Time Grooves

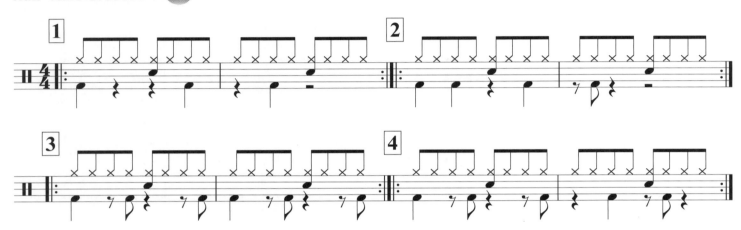

Half-Time Transitions

The next step is "entering" and "exiting" the half-time groove from the original groove. The use of a simple fill can help bridge these two grooves. At first this may present some coordination issues, but they can easily be resolved by repetition. Try using any of the previous half-time grooves in the B section of the following example.

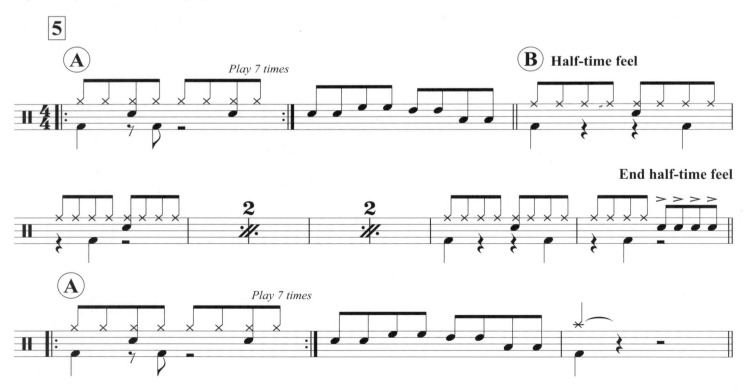

"HALFWAY HOME"

Here is a funk groove that moves into a half-time feel.

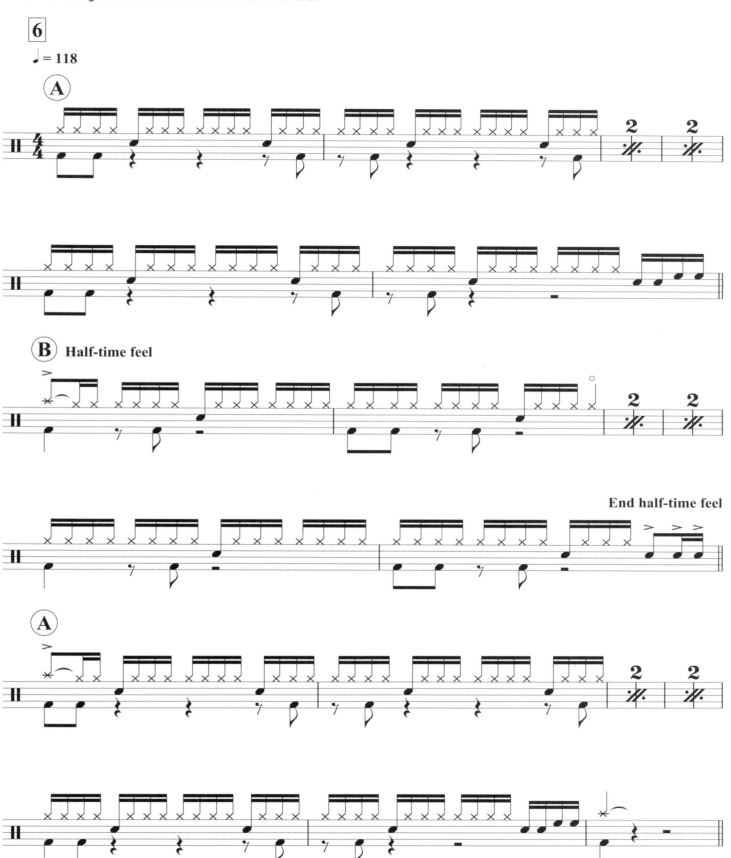

"SIDEWALK SHUFFLE"

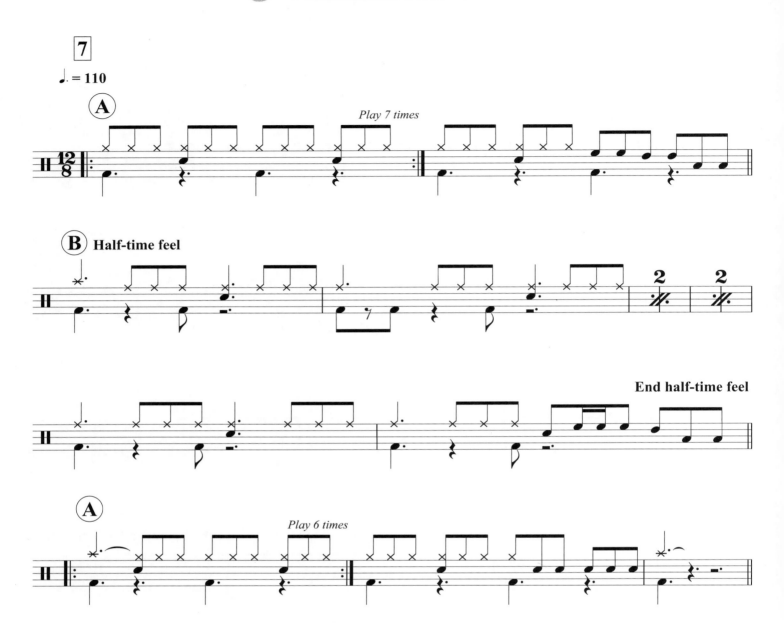

LESSON 20: 16TH RESTS

QUICK TIP – Singing or counting 16th-note subdivisions while you play can help you feel the spaces within the beat.

The 16th rest (𝄾) can create many interesting syncopated rhythms. Check out the rhythms that are made as we move the 16th rest around to different parts of the beat.

(1) e & ah

1 (e) & ah

1 e (&) ah

1 e & (ah)

Combining three 16th notes can create one dotted 8th note (♪.) or one dotted 8th rest (𝄾.):

1 - e - & - ah

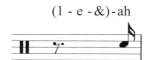
(1 - e - &) - ah

1 - e - & - ah

1 - e - & - ah

New Rhythms Exercise

Try the following lines with some of these new rhythms. Notice that the written stickings are derived from a "flow sticking system," where each leading group of four 16ths starts with the right hand.

Bass and Snare Groove Variations

Following are patterns that make use of some of our newest 16th rhythms. The "A" examples will use an alternating 16th-note pattern on the hi-hat, while the "B" examples contain an 8th-note pattern on the ride cymbal (or hi-hat, if you prefer). Notice how the bass drum lines up with the hand subdivision. **Note:** on the audio demonstration track, only the "A" examples are played.

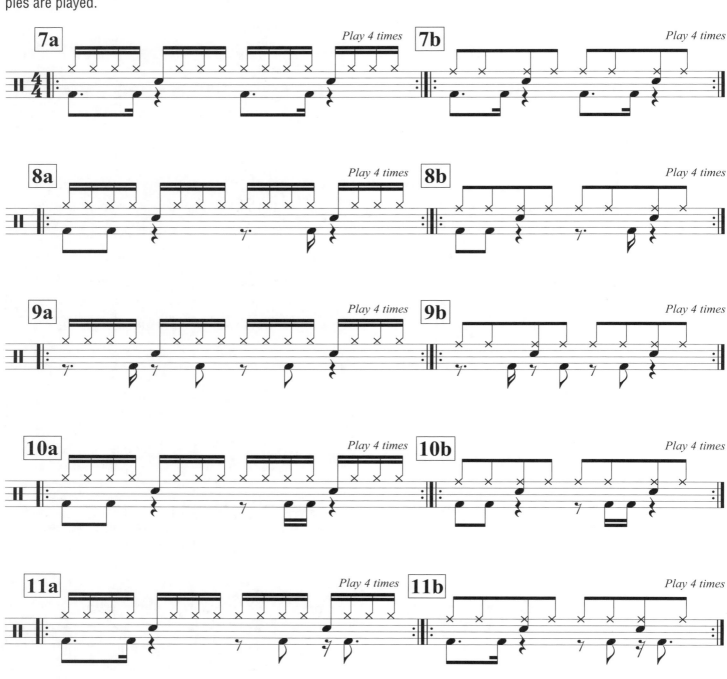

"POCKET CHANGE"

LESSON 21: SYNCOPATED FILLS

QUICK TIP – In funk music, drum fills tend to be shorter in length because the music is very groove-oriented.

With knowledge of 8th- and 16th-note rhythms, fills with more syncopation can now be used. This will give the drummer many more creative ideas for adding rhythmical interest. Here are some examples:

Two-Beat Fills

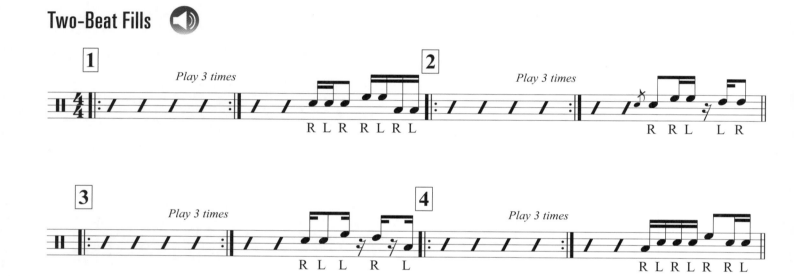

One-Bar Fills

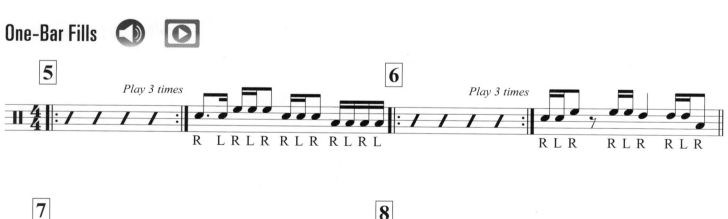

Syncopated Grooves

Adding an extra snare drum note to the existing backbeats can make some grooves even more funky!

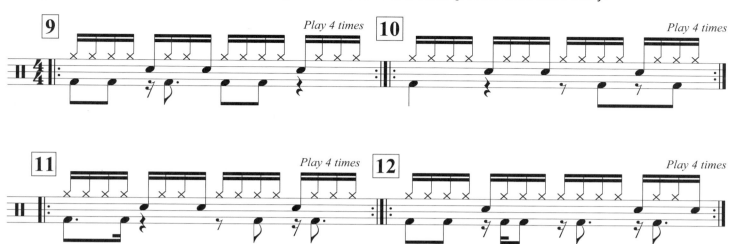

"PHAT MONKEY"

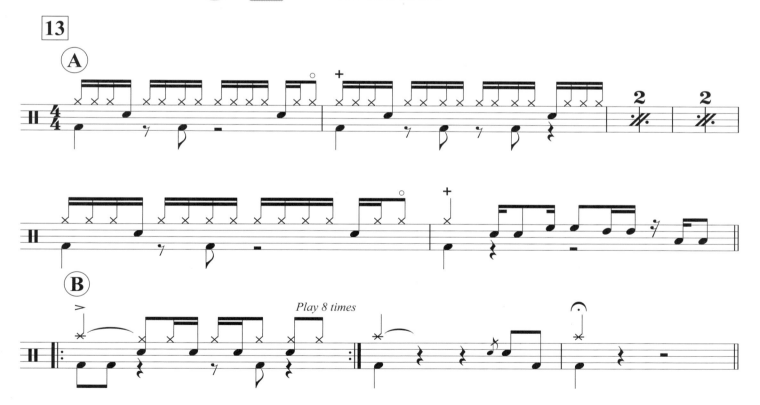

LESSON 22: FUNK GROOVES

> **QUICK TIP** – Opening the hi-hat during a 16th-note groove is a great way to break up the beat. It starts to sound funky because of the moving 16th-note accents.

Playing 16th-note grooves with the right hand as the ostinato can become challenging if the player does not have adequate technique. A basic technical foundation is necessary for these grooves to be played. Remember to slow the tempo down accordingly and use a relaxed stroke. Try some of these funk grooves.

Funk Grooves

Note: on the audio demonstration track, only the "A" examples are played.

Opening the hi-hat within right-handed 16th-note grooves can really add some variety to the beat. Remember to space the hi-hat cymbals apart enough so the open sound can be audible. The tempo and rhythm will most likely determine if you should use the "heel-toe" technique or the "bounce" technique. Here are some basic hi-hat variations you can practice with the simple groove listed below them. Open and close the hi-hat in tempo.

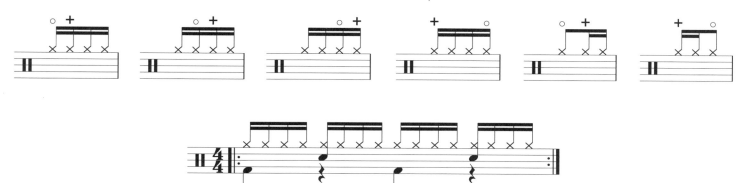

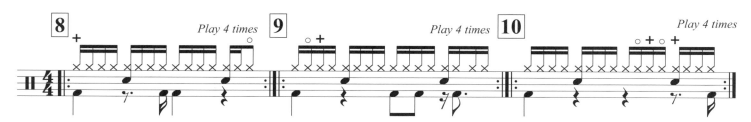

Hi-Hat Variations

Now try these grooves with some hi-hat variations.

🔊 "SHARE MY GROOVE"

LESSON 23: DISPLACED BACKBEATS

QUICK TIP – The main drummers for James Brown included Clyde Stubblefield, Jabo Starks, and Melvin Parker. These three are largely responsible for creating and perfecting the funk style.

In the 1970s, funk and rock started to merge together, creating a new spread of syncopated grooves. These types of grooves commonly used shifting accents to give the music a fresh sound. Typically, the snare drum is played on beats 2 and 4 (the backbeats), but during this time period, the snare drum began to be "displaced" to other beats. Here are some examples of this.

Displaced Snare Grooves

Note: on the audio demonstration track, the "A" examples (ride cymbal grooves) are played through first, followed by the "B" examples (hi-hat grooves).

Some of the most influential leaders of this "greasy" groove were the drummers for the James Brown Band. Here's a look at one of the most popular grooves:

"HOT SWEAT"

TIME TO GET FUNKY

Any drummer can get funky and create some beat combinations with the 16th-note syncopated rhythms you have learned. Use any mixture of examples 6–20 below with one or more "beat 2 and 4" combos from A–E. You can come up with hundreds of beats.

Funky Combos

The audio demonstration features different combinations of the following one-beat rhythms. The full example shown below them is a sample combination of these.

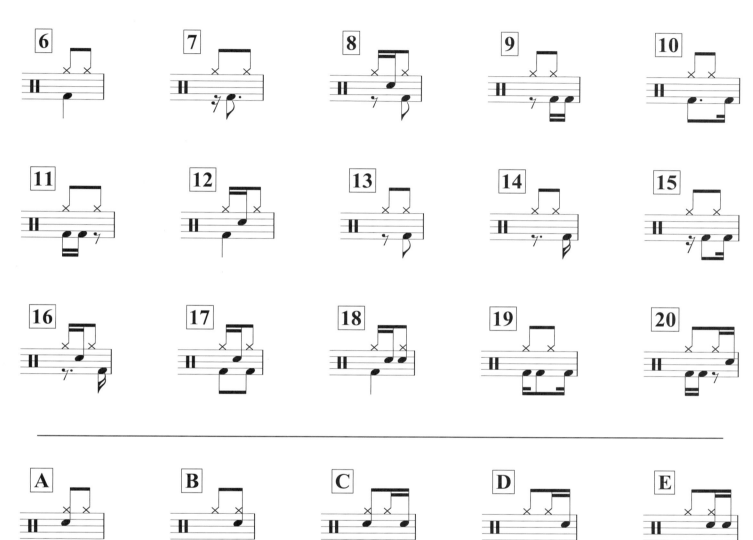

Combo Example:

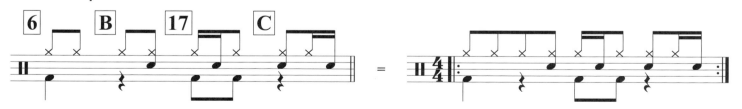

> **Rimshot –** played by striking the drumhead and rim at the same time. This technique is used very often for playing the backbeats in certain styles of music. It is notated with an "X" notehead.

 **"BRING ME THERE"**

This tune includes cross-stick and rimshots.

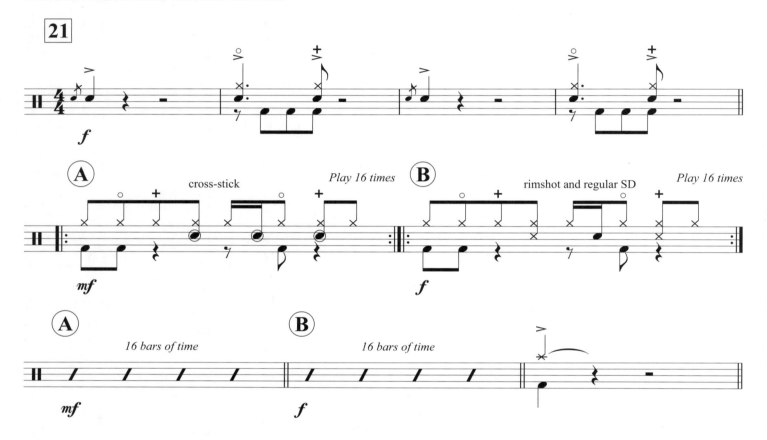

LESSON 24: GHOST NOTES

QUICK TIP – Some of the most notable masters of ghost-note drumming include Harvey Mason, Bernard Purdie, Steve Gadd, and David Garibaldi.

UNDERSTANDING GHOST NOTES

Ghost notes are a very big part of funk and R&B music (rhythm and blues). The term "ghosted" refers to notes played but not always heard. In other words, they are a bit softer compared to the main notes or accents. Using ghost notes can really give your drumming a special feel and unique quality. They are played at a lighter volume level with a lower stick height, similar to playing unaccented taps. Playing the unaccented notes lower really gives this style of music its character; they are more "felt" than heard. In order to play ghost notes, you will need a proficient level of control to execute unaccented notes directly after an accent. Try the following sticking on a single surface and then move the right-hand accents around the drums while keeping the other notes low.

$$\overset{>}{R}\ L\ \overset{>}{R}\ L\ L\ \overset{>}{R}\ L\ L$$

Also try paradiddle sticking:

$$\overset{>}{R}\ L\ R\ R\ \overset{>}{L}\ R\ L\ L$$

In this chapter we will help identify the ghosted notes by placing them in parentheses. Remember to make a nice contrast between the accented notes and unaccented notes.

Ghost-Note Exercise

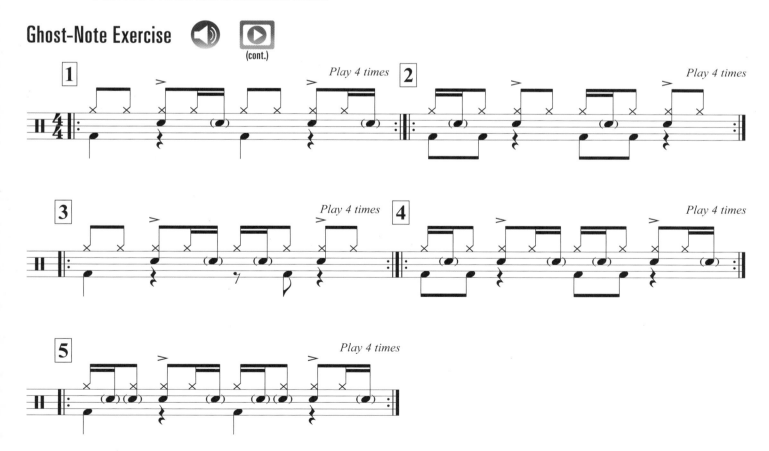

Try a few hands-only grooves that contain a few more ghosted notes.

Ghost Hands Exercise 1

Ghost Hands Exercise 2

The bass drum is added starting at Example 9B and Example 10 is a paradiddle groove.

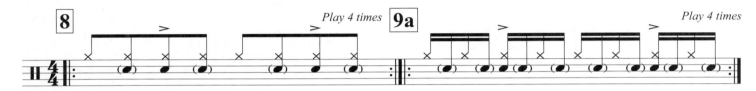

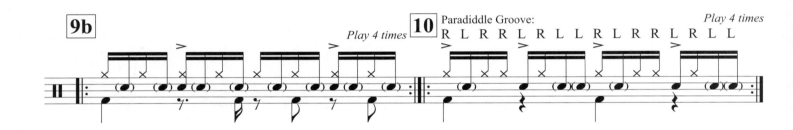

"GHOST BAND"

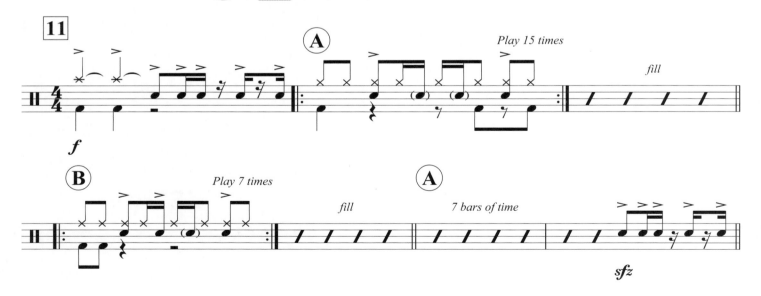

LESSON 25: JAZZ COMPING

QUICK TIP – Drummers in the early years of the swing era did almost all comping exclusively on the snare drum. Bass drum became more utilized by drummers such as Kenny Clarke, Art Blakey, Roy Haynes, Max Roach, and Shelly Manne.

In jazz drumming, "comping" is one of the most essential elements. "Comping" comes from the word "compliment" or "accompany." So the drummer is trying to compliment and accompany the ride cymbal and the music. This will provide interest to the groove, add variety to the time, and foster communication with the other musicians.

Comping Exercise

Let's play a steady ride cymbal and hi-hat pattern while introducing some snare and bass drum comp figures. Please keep in mind that all rhythmic figures are played in a triplet feel, or swing feel.

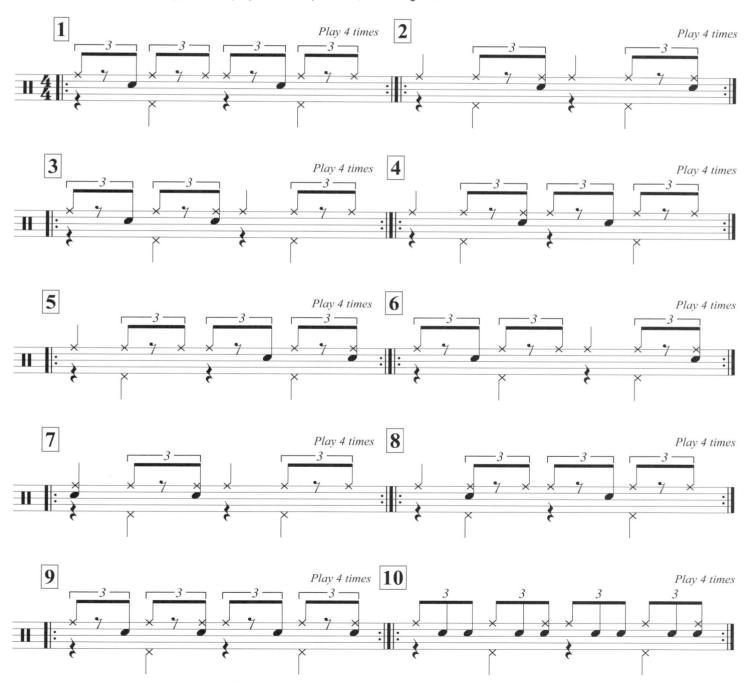

Below are the four basic jazz **articulations**, representing the degree to which notes are separated or connected:

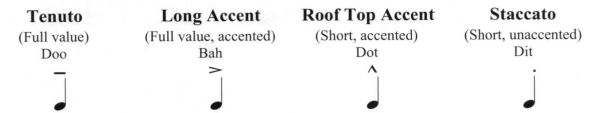

Tenuto	Long Accent	Roof Top Accent	Staccato
(Full value)	(Full value, accented)	(Short, accented)	(Short, unaccented)
Doo	Bah	Dot	Dit

Isolated Comp Rhythms

Now let's try playing the isolated comp figures. Visualize the ride cymbal and hi-hat pattern in your head while playing the written rhythms. Remember to swing all 8th notes. Here are some of the most commonly used:

"THANKS FOR THE COMPLIMENT"

While continuing the jazz ride pattern with beats 2 and 4 on the hi-hat, play each variation below four times and proceed. Feel free to mix up the snare and bass drum, as heard on the audio demonstration track.

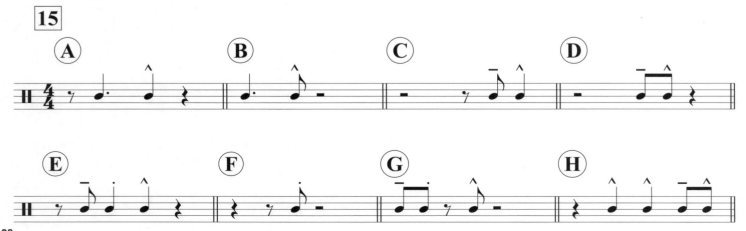

LESSON 26: JAZZ STICKINGS

QUICK TIP – Practicing accents within a triplet jazz base is very helpful for creating new fill ideas.

The rhythmic flow of jazz drumming is centered on the triplet-based 8th note. The drummer must start with a single surface, such as the snare drum, before moving around the drumset. Creating a fluid motion of legato strokes will be helpful when playing fills, set-ups, and solos (you'll learn more about set-ups and solos in the coming lessons).

Jazz Sticking Exercise

Two sticking methods should be used for the following exercises:

1. Hand to Hand: R L R L R L

2. Right-Hand Lead: the right hand plays all of the accents and the left hand fills in between.

Add soft, "feathered" bass drum quarter notes with the right foot and hi-hat on 2 and 4 with the left foot, and play with a swing feel. After you're comfortable playing the exercises on the snare, change up the accents by playing them on different drums, as heard on the audio demonstration track.

Now try to play a continuous flow of 8th-note triplets around the drumset using different surfaces and sticking patterns. The goal here is to develop a smooth flow using triplets around the drums.

Smooth Triplet Exercise

Focus on playing smooth, continuous triplets around the drums.

LESSON 27: CHART INTERPRETATION

QUICK TIP – Composers will differ on how they notate ensemble and section figures. The figures can be written above the staff, in the staff, or even like drum notation.

UNDERSTANDING CHART NOTATION

Quite often when a drummer reads a chart, the majority of what he or she plays is not on the printed music. The drummer has a unique responsibility to decide what to play from the information given on the chart. This is referred to as **interpretation**.

The main role of the drummer is to provide solid time and establish an appropriate groove (or feel) for the music. The drummer may also play some of the ensemble or section figures that are usually written above the staff, or on the staff (sometimes with larger notes called slash notation). Composers differ on how they notate these figures. Here are three different examples of what the same drum chart might look like:

Written Above the Staff:

Written on the Staff (in Slash Notation):

Written as Drum Notation:

But, what happens during rests? When reading a drumset chart, a rest means one of two things:

1. Actually rest and do *not* play, or

2. Insert a fill

Most often the word "fill" is not found in music, and the drummer must use his or her intuition to decide when one should be played. Main accents are often notated and fills can be used tastefully in a rest. Longer fill sections are usually marked in the music and some may just say "solo."

How to interpret figures and rests? This is not a simple answer, but there are definitely some guidelines that will be discussed in the following lessons. Sometimes it is best to just play some simple reinforced rhythms on the snare drum. And then, after you get more comfortable, use different drums and cymbals to add color.

Drum Chart:

Simple Reinforcement:

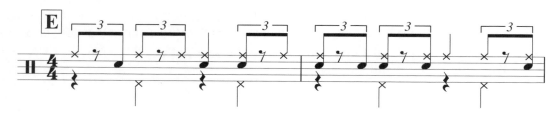

Add Other Drums for More Variation:

Following are several two-measure examples to practice. Each is jazz-based and played with a swing feel.

LESSON 28: SET-UPS

> **QUICK TIP –** Some of the most notable jazz big band leaders include Chick Webb, Duke Ellington, Gene Krupa, Benny Goodman, Count Basie, and Buddy Rich.

SHORT AND LONG NOTES

In big band music, the drummer should know how to properly play short notes and long notes. **Short notes** are commonly played with the snare drum (or bass drum, or even choked hi-hat cymbal) against the standard ride pattern. Short notes can occur on both downbeats and upbeats, but rarely require a set-up.

Short-Note Figures

Here are a few variations with short-note figures:

Long notes are usually tied, creating a value greater than a quarter note. They are played on a cymbal and bass drum (or snare drum) at the same time. Long notes usually have a **set-up** into the figure. In other words, you are playing a small fill that leads into an ensemble entrance that you literally "kick." Let's try a few exercises using the snare drum to "set up," and then the bass drum and crash to "kick" the ensemble figure.

Long-Note Figures

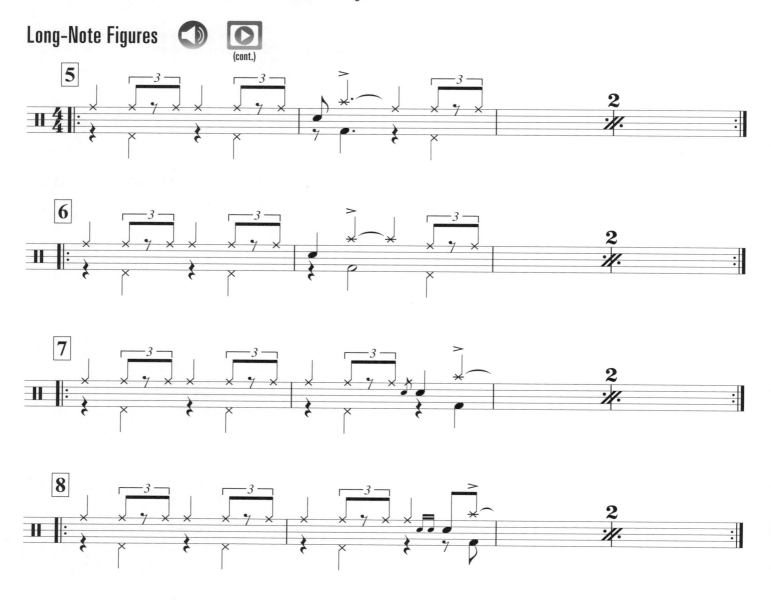

Most commonly played set-up figures include the quarter note (lines 5–6), flam (line 7), and ruff (line 8). A **ruff** is like a flam but played with more than one grace note. The stick is allowed to bounce for the grace notes.

Several things can determine the kind of fill or set-up that should be played.

Slow Tempo Set-Up

16th notes work well for slow-tempo fills and set-ups.

Medium Tempo Set-Up

Triplets work well for medium-tempo fills and set-ups.

Up-Tempo Set-Up

Simple, one-count, downbeat fills and set-ups work well for **up-tempo** music (fast tempos).

"GO GET IT"

LESSON 29: LONG VS. SHORT SOUNDS

> **QUICK TIP –** In jazz-style music, quarter notes are usually played staccato, while 8th notes are usually played legato.

Another important aspect of chart reading is the ability of the drummer to match the note lengths of the ensemble with those of the drumset. Learning to match these articulations (note shape) means the drummer has to think like a horn player.

Also refer to Lesson 25 for additional information on articulations.

Short Articulations *(Might use snare drum, rimshot, hi-hat choke):*

Staccato (·)

Marcato (housetop, ^)

Short Note Value

Long Articulations *(Might use cymbal crashes):*

Tenuto (—)

Tie (⌒)

Long Note Value

Ensemble Exercise 1

Let's try a few examples of kicking isolated figures with various articulations. You should be able to "sing" these lines as well as play them. Check out Lesson 25 to review the syllables used to count and verbalize jazz articulations.

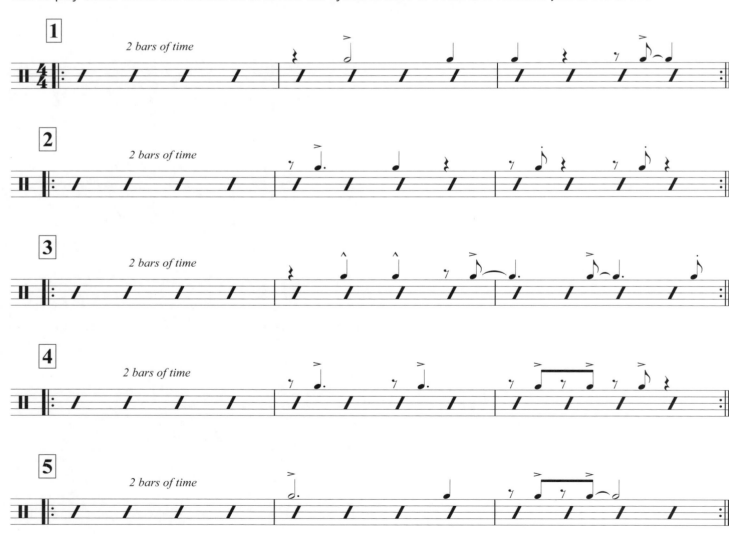

Ensemble Exercise 2

"The 8th-Note Rule" is a general guideline for deciding what notes to play when there is more than just a single 8th note by itself. When an 8th note is standing by itself (as in lines 1–5) with nothing after it, it will usually be played as an accent. If the 8th note is followed by another note (or more), it becomes a "filler" note before the accent (see lines 6–9). An exception to this rule would occur when there are four 8th notes together. In this case, you would accent the first and last notes (see lines 10 and 11).

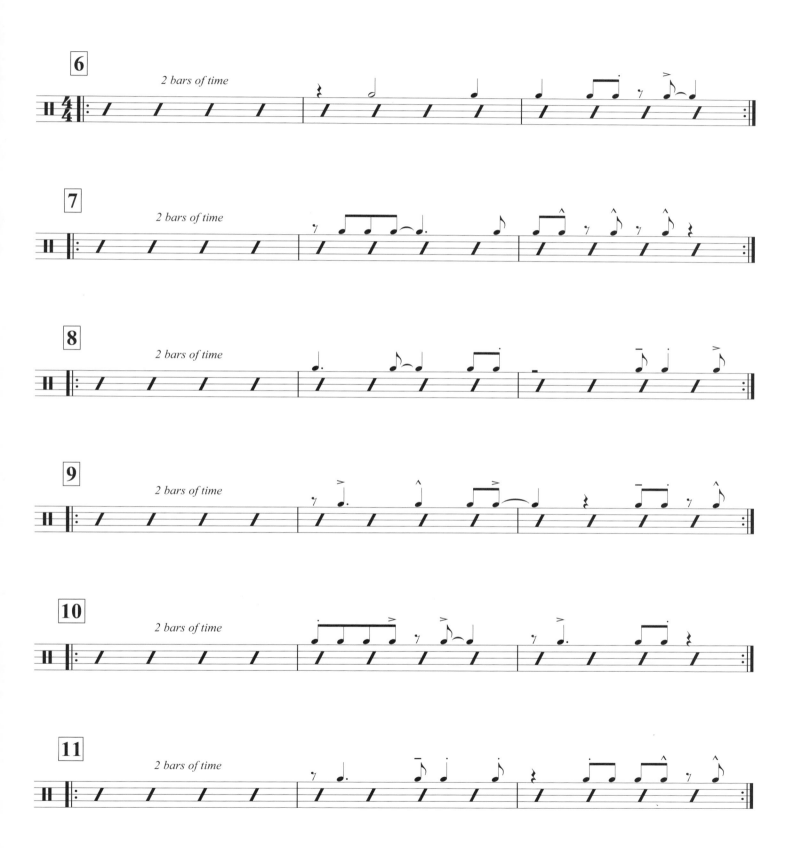

"SWINGIN' JOE"

In the following song, you'll see a new routing direction: **D.C. al Fine**. "D.C." stands for the Italian phrase "da capo," meaning "from the beginning." This direction tells you to return to the beginning of the song and play up to the word "Fine," which means "end."

LESSON 30: DRUM SOLOING

> **QUICK TIP** – One of the best ways to learn how to solo is by transcribing solos yourself. This will help you develop a solo vocabulary.

The two words "drum solo" can bring fear to drummers with limited experience. A drum solo can range in length from one bar to eight bars or longer. Sometimes a drum solo is used to help transition into another section, or even to help change the mood from the current groove. Every drummer should have a library of simple one-bar phrases like these:

One-Bar Solo Phrases

Play all the lines with a swing feel, except for line 8.

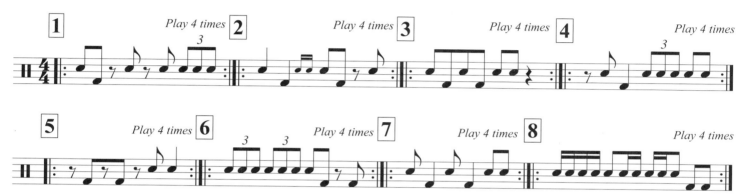

Creating a Drum Solo

Here are some tips for creating drum solos in a jazz style with a swing feel. **Note:** on the accompanying audio, the following examples are played in continuous succession across one track.

Repetition

Repetition means taking a musical phrase or section of music and repeating exactly the same phrase or altering the idea. Play four bars of time and then solo for four bars. This is commonly known as "trading fours."

Orchestration

Experiment using different drums, cymbals, rimshots, etc.

Dynamics

Using different levels of dynamics will give your solo energy and even more personality.

Add Rests

A really easy way to add variety to your solo is to insert some space by using rests.

Add Rests Within the Phrase

Embellishments

Embellish means to "decorate" the music. This can be achieved by using accents, flams, ruffs, rimshots, etc.

"LUCKY SEVEN"
(cont.)

The final exercise is a short tune with some solo breaks. Take note that there will be no click on the audio tracks during the solo. Therefore, you must keep a steady pulse and re-enter in time.

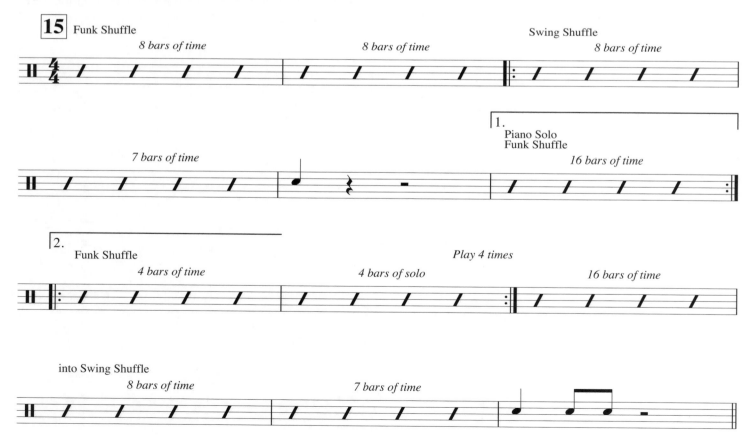

LESSON 31: JAZZ CHARTS

QUICK TIP – A drummer uses the trial and error method when sight reading a piece of music.
It is better to "underplay" than "overplay" the first time through.

Following are two sample jazz charts containing many of the concepts you have learned thus far.

"JAZZ CHART 1"

"JAZZ CHART 2"

LESSON 32: ROCK/FUNK CHARTS

QUICK TIP – Less is sometimes more! Simple grooves and simple fills can often be more appropriate than busy playing. Use your ears to make smart musical choices.

ROCK/FUNK CHART READING

When playing a chart in the style of rock or funk, there are a few things to remember:

1. Use any written idea or reference of the desired groove to help determine what you might play.

2. Listen to the bass player and rhythm section for style and rhythmic ostinato.

3. Funk fills usually set up the downbeat of the next measure, but sometimes a funk fill can end on a syncopated figure as seen below:

Funk Fill 1

Funk Fill 2

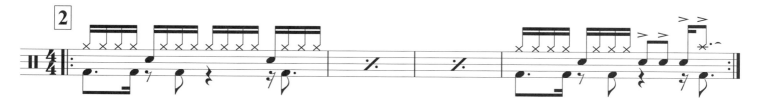

4. The drummer does not have to play *everything* they see on a chart. But they must identify the different roles he or she will play throughout the music. What is the primary groove? Does the groove change? Are there any soloists? What figures should I catch? When/if should I go to hi-hat vs. ride cymbal?

Funk Chart Exercise

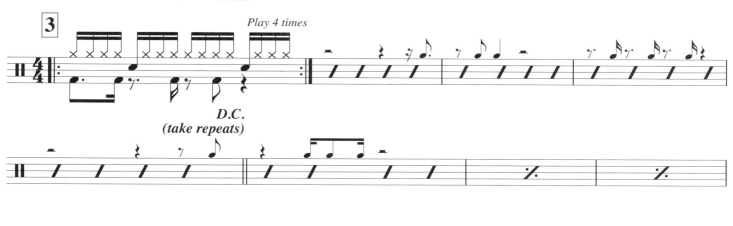

As you look at example 4, some choices have to be made about how you are going to catch the figures starting in measure 5. Many of these figures can picked up within the groove. In other words, keep the backbeat on 2 and 4 as much as possible while playing some of the cues with bass drum, hi-hat, or other parts of the kit. Using the snare drum to kick many of the rhythms will prevent the groove from flowing evenly.

"ROCK CHART 1"

LESSON 33: BRUSH PLAYING

QUICK TIP – Some masters of brush playing are Ed Thigpen, Philly Joe Jones, Jeff Hamilton, and Clayton Cameron.

Playing with brushes is another skill often used by jazz drummers. This distinct sound can commonly be heard in standard tempo songs, but especially in slow tempo ballads. Brushes can provide a warm, smooth, and fluid mood at lower volumes and at all tempos. Unlike playing with sticks, brush playing requires a type of sustained (constant) motion.

Brush Pattern 1

This basic brush pattern can be used at most tempos. The left hand will circle clockwise in half notes starting around the 10 o'clock position on beats 1 and 3. Arrive at 4 to 5 o'clock on beats 2 and 4. Try to keep the left hand smooth and legato. The right hand will play the jazz ride pattern by gently tapping on the drumhead from the right (on beats 1 and 3) to the left (on beats 2 and 4). The hands will actually cross on beats 2 and 4, but keep the left-hand sound smooth and consistent.

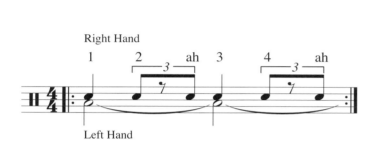

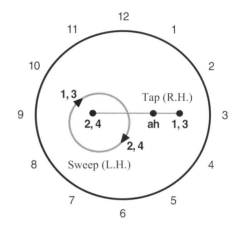

"MISS JONES"

This next tune is a medium swing played with brushes. You'll see a new marking in the last few measures of this chart: "rit." This stands for **ritardando** and means to gradually slow down.

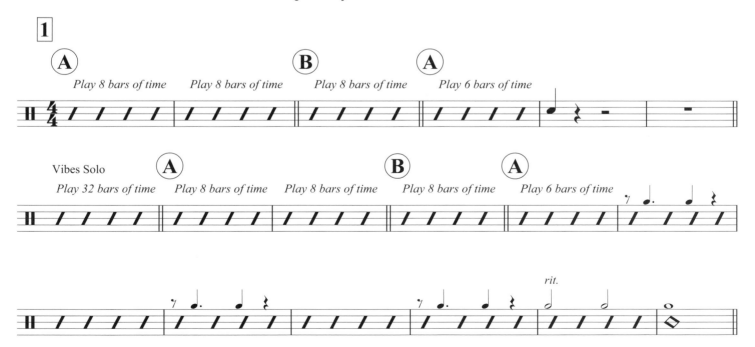

Brush Pattern 2

This ballad pattern can be used for very slow tempos. Practice each hand separately starting at the 12 o'clock position and brush a circle in quarter notes. The left hand moves clockwise while the right hand brushes counterclockwise. Try a slight push of the brush into the head on each downbeat to help establish some weight for the quarter-note pulse. When you have achieved a consistent legato motion, put the hands together. Each hand circles in quarter notes while coming towards the other on the downbeats.

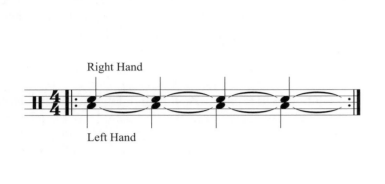
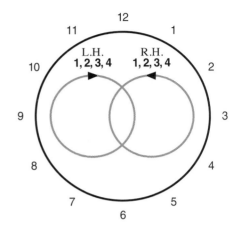

Brush Pattern 2 Variation

This works well for a swing ballad tempo. The left hand circles quarter notes while the right hand plays the jazz ride pattern.

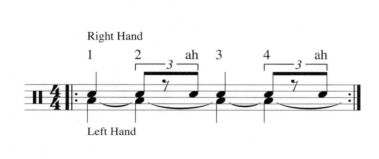
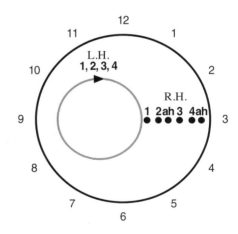

 "VALENTINE'S DAY"

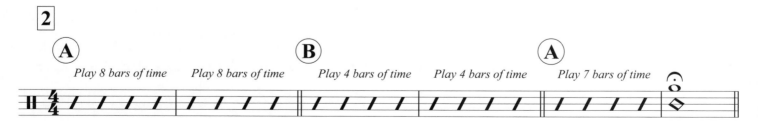

LESSON 34: COUNTRY DRUMMING

QUICK TIP – The "Nashville Number System" is a common system used by Nashville musicians when reading and writing chord charts. Each chord change in a tune has a corresponding number.

COUNTRY VARIATIONS

Country is a type of American music that developed in the southern part of the United States in the late 1800s. Originating with Western swing, "honky tonk" style, the Grand Ole Opry, country shuffle, country pop, the "outlaw movement," Opryland, country rock, the "Nashville sound," and exploding into modern country.

Modern country most often uses a shuffle (or straight 8th-note) groove.

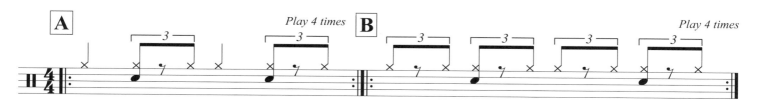

Country Shuffle

Here is a shuffle using a brush with the right hand on the snare and cross-stick (also called **side-stick** or **rim knock**) with the left hand on beats 2 and 4:

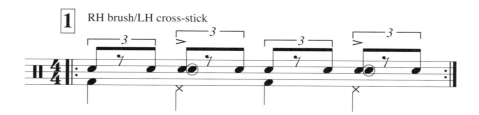

Traditional Shuffle

Here is a more traditional country shuffle, followed by the same beat with a half-time feel.

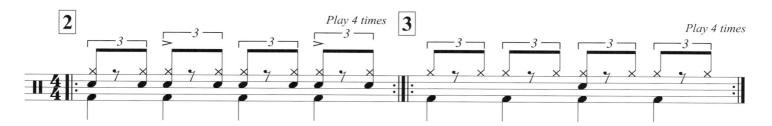

Country rock and pop includes more straight 8th-note beats and features many snare and bass drum patterns similar to those found in rock and funk music. However, a country groove may have a creative approach to an old idea.

Country Rock/Pop

Playing a contrasting sound on beat 4 can add some texture and/or energy to a country pattern, as seen in these next two examples.

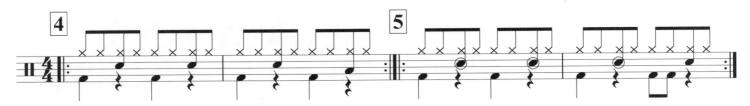

Snare Drum Pattern 1

Play the right hand hi-hat pattern on the snare drum.

Snare Drum Pattern 2

Now try 16ths on the snare drum.

"BIG TEX"

LESSON 35: HIP-HOP/DANCE BEATS

QUICK TIP – The common trademark of hip-hop music is the swing feel. However, most half-time feels in hip-hop style are usually played straight rather than swung.

Hip-hop began in New York City in the late 1970s and became extremely popular in the 1990s. In this style, all of the 16th notes should have a slight swing. As a result of the mixture of rock and funk grooves, the possible variations are almost endless.

Hip-Hop Grooves

Remember to slightly swing the 16th notes.

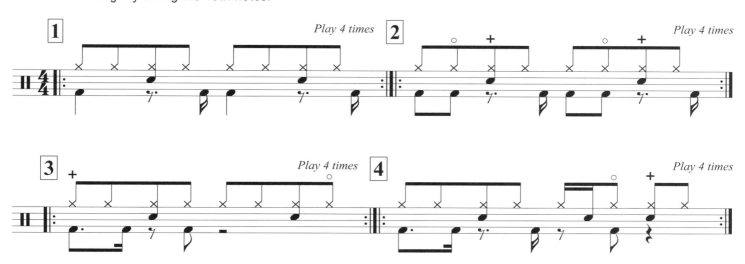

Also play the above variations with alternated, shuffled 16th notes on the hi-hat.

"GET READY"

(cont.)

Another type of groove that spawned from a combination of hip-hop and disco music was house dance music. All of these beats were played around the tempo of 120 bpm, similar to disco. Use of the open hi-hat and "four on the floor" is also a big characteristic of house.

House Grooves

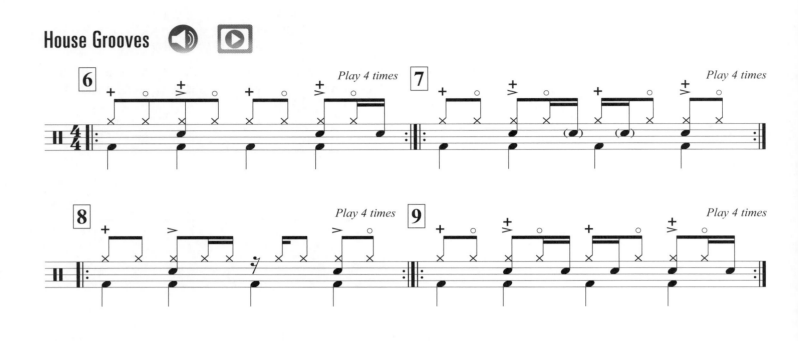

"HOUSE MONEY"

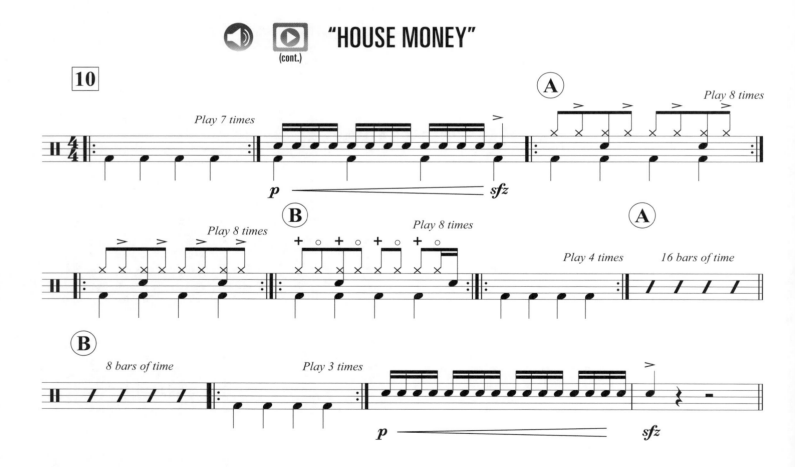

LESSON 36: CALYPSO/SOCA

QUICK TIP – "Day-O (The Banana Boat Song)" is a classic calypso recording made by Harry Belafonte and based on a traditional Jamaican folk song.

Caribbean music is a combination of many different musical cultures. The rhythms and instruments (like steel drum) are often referred to as "island music." Two of the most commonly played styles within this genre include **calypso** and **soca**. The calypso beat usually has a bit more syncopation in the bass drum pattern. Here are a few variations:

Calypso Variations

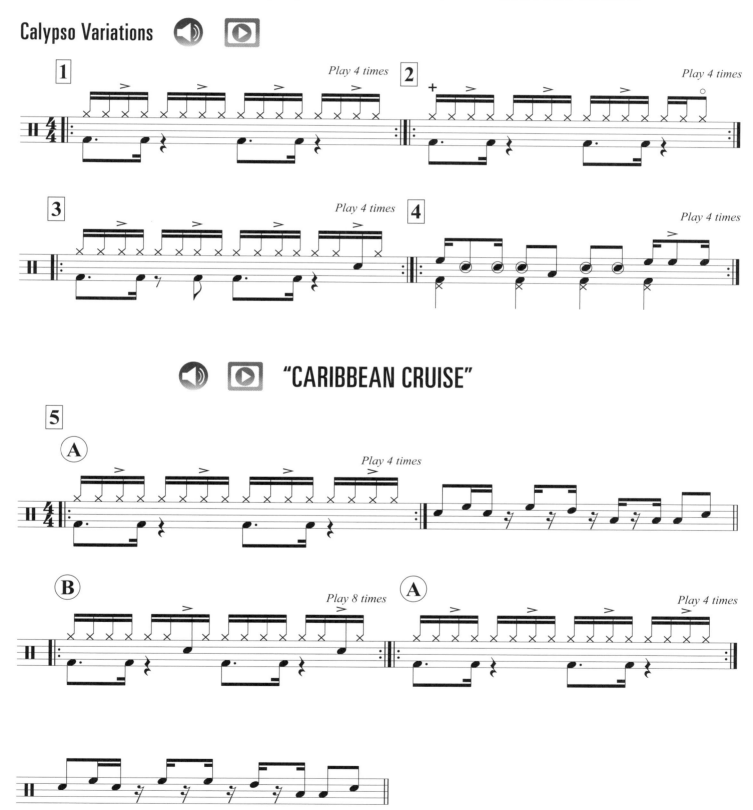

"CARIBBEAN CRUISE"

In the 1970s, disco was the soul of American music. The mixture of disco and calypso melded into soca. This style features a high-energy groove that gets its pulse from driving quarter notes on the bass drum with the hi-hat opening on each upbeat.

Soca Grooves

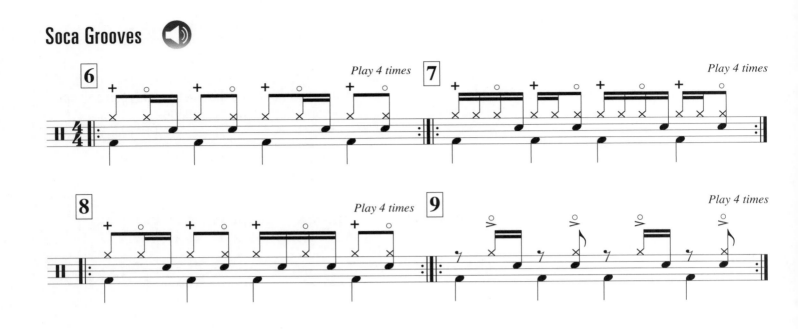

"SOCA SPIRIT"

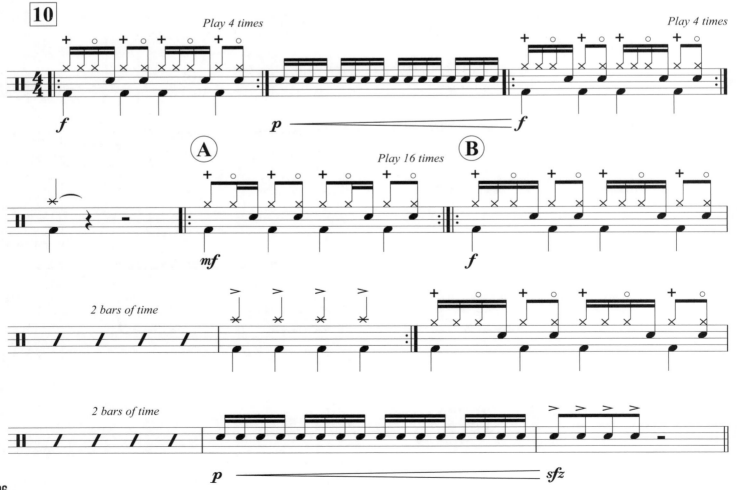

LESSON 37: AFRO-CUBAN STYLES

QUICK TIP – One of the most recognized cha-cha grooves in Latin and American pop music is entitled "Oye Como Va"—written by Tito Puente and famously redone by Santana.

The term **Afro-Cuban** refers to the blending of music from Africa, Cuba, Puerto Rico, and the Dominican Republic. The merging of all these cultures resulted in many new forms of music. Some of these will be discussed in the next few lessons.

CLAVE

The pulse of Afro-Cuban music is the **clave**, which means "key" in Spanish. The clave is both an instrument and a rhythm. As the cymbal ride pattern is to jazz, the clave is to Afro-Cuban music. There are two measures in a clave pattern. One measure has two notes and the other has three notes. Claves are two pieces of wood that are struck together. This rhythm can also be played on almost any part of the drumset.

2:3 Clave Patterns

The following exercises feature the 2:3 clave rhythm, with two notes in the first measure and three in the second. A **rhumba** is a popular Cuban dance where the clave includes a slight displacement of the third note (beat 4) in the second measure. Each clave below is played alone first and then along with 8th notes on the hi-hat.

2:3 Son Clave

2:3 Rhumba Clave

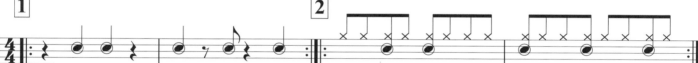

3:2 Clave Patterns
(cont.)

Next up is the 3:2 clave rhythm, with three notes in the first measure and two in the second. Each clave is played alone first and then along with 8th notes on the hi-hat.

3:2 Son Clave

3:2 Rhumba Clave

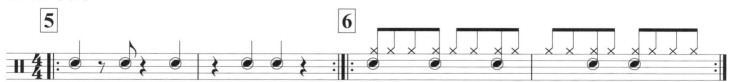

TUMBAO

Tumbao is a repeated rhythm that is usually played by the bass player and/or conga player in Afro-Cuban music. The drum-set player can reinforce this with the bass drum.

Tumbao Patterns

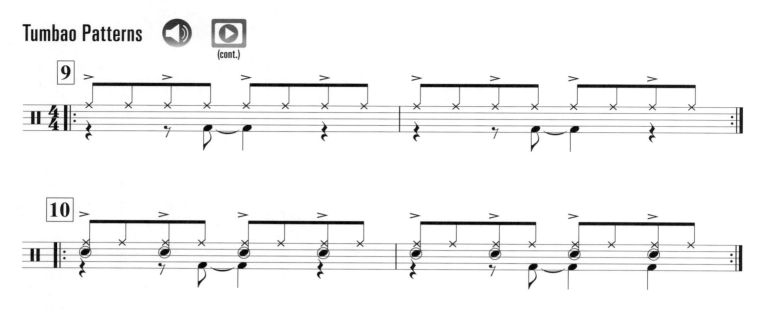

CASCARA

Another important Afro-Cuban rhythm is called the **cascara**. When used on the drumset, this rhythm can be played with the right hand on the closed hi-hat, ride cymbal, rim or shell of floor tom, cowbell, or the cymbal bell.

Cascara Patterns

Here is the basic cascara rhythm, also shown with clave and tumbao.

Cascara

With Clave

With Tumbao

CHA-CHA

The **cha-cha** comes from the cha-cha-cha, an Afro-Cuban salsa dance. It is very similar to a mambo but played at a slower tempo. (The mambo is covered in the following lesson.) The cha-cha groove starts with a quarter-note cowbell rhythm and 8th notes played by the guiro (or on the hi-hat). In the following variations, the cowbell part can be played on the ride cymbal bell (line 14) or with the cross-stick technique (line 15–16).

Cha-Cha Patterns

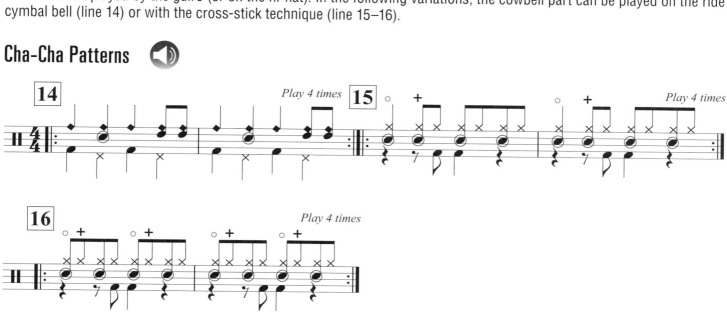

"LA BAHAMA"

LESSON 38:
MORE AFRO-CUBAN STYLES

QUICK TIP — The groove of Afro-Cuban music comes from the slight swing feel that is characteristic in this style. It can sometimes be in between 8th notes and triplets. Listening to music of this style will help you learn to capture the authentic feel.

MAMBO ▶

The **mambo** may be the most popular of all of the Afro-Cuban musical styles. Most often a mambo is performed with several percussionists, so a drumset player has a challenge to cover these parts with only four limbs. The right hand usually covers the mambo bell pattern, the left hand covers the conga pattern, the bass drum plays the tumbao pattern (or variation), and the hi-hat can play on beats 1 and 3, or 2 and 4. The mambo is a two-measure pattern that is based on the son clave, starting with the two or three pattern.

Traditional Mambo 🔊

Mambo Variation

110

The term **salsa** refers to a form or style of Afro-Cuban music that was actually created in the United States in the 1970s. Like the mambo, the primary instruments are congas, timbales, bongos, claves, and cowbells. Here is the basic salsa form:

Intro – Verse – Montuno *(starts with piano solo)* **– Mambo – Verse – Outro**

🔊 "PASS THE PICANTE"

SONGO

Unlike any of the previously mentioned Afro-Cuban grooves, the **songo** was actually conceived with the drumset rhythm first and then additional percussion instruments were added. Songo rhythms are built from a mixture of various Afro-Cuban musical styles. The right hand usually plays a steady pulse, the bass drum plays the tumbao rhythm, and the snare fills in with syncopated notes (some ghosted as well).

Songo Patterns

Standard Songo Groove

Songo Groove Variations

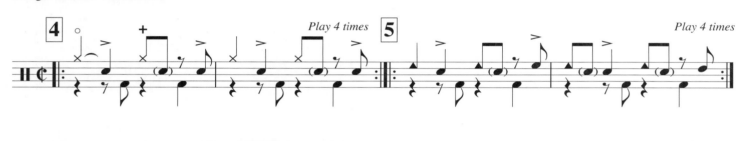

"CUBAN DANCE"

In the following song, you'll see a new routing direction: ***D.S. al Fine***. "D.S." stands for the Italian phrase "dal segno," meaning "from the sign." This direction tells you to return to the sign (𝄋) and play up to the "Fine."

112

LESSON 39: BRAZILIAN STYLES

QUICK TIP – Samba batucada refers to percussion rhythms of the parade (street) samba from the annual Carnaval in Rio de Janeiro. Some of the batucada instruments include repinique, tamborim, pandeiro, caixa, surdo, cuica, and agogo.

BOSSA NOVA

Bossa nova may be the most popular Latin groove originating from Brazil. It is much more subtle and laid back compared to other types of Latin grooves. A lighter approach and touch is recommended for this style. It should be played in a smooth and seamless manner.

Bossa Nova Patterns

Usually, a medium-tempo bossa nova is played with cross-stick. There are many variations of the cross-stick pattern that can be played. The bass drum has a repeated rhythm throughout. First, try playing 8th notes on the hi-hat with the right hand along with the repeated bass drum rhythm, and then add the cross-stick patterns as shown in the following examples:

Main Pattern

Bossa Nova A (hi-hat)

Bossa Nova B (ride cymbal)

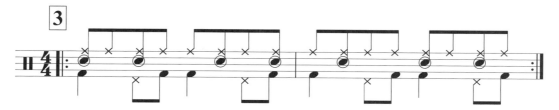

"BIG BOSS OF NOVA"

In the following song, you'll see a new routing direction: ***D.S. al Coda***. As you learned earlier, "D.S." tells you to return to the sign (𝄋) in the chart. Next, "al Coda" directs you to play up to the "To Coda" sign (⨁). When you reach it, you should go directly to where the other similar coda sign is located and play to the end of the piece.

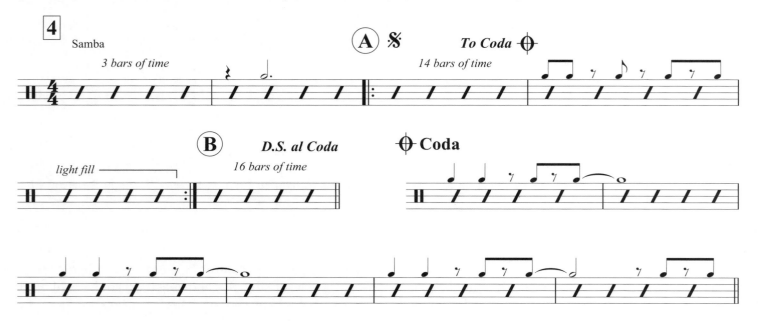

SAMBA

Samba is another popular rhythm from Brazil. This musical style comes from the many samba bands that perform at the Carnaval Festival each year in Rio. These bands are filled with many musicians that contribute to the exciting and hypnotic grooves that fill the air. The percussion instruments found in the samba band include the surdo, the caixa, the repenique, the tamborim, and the ganza (shaker). Each of these instruments play a specific rhythm which all blend together for an incredible energy and excitement. Since there are so many instruments and rhythms going on, a drumset player has some freedom and creativity to choose which ones to play on the set to create this type of groove.

Similar to the bossa nova, the bass drum also has a repeated pattern throughout. Here is the foot pattern:

Samba Patterns

Slow to Medium Samba

Jazz Samba

Samba Variation

Play 4 times

Fast Samba

"SUMMER SAMBA"

ENCORE #3

Congratulations for making it through Book 2 of the *Hal Leonard Drumset Method!* Here are two full song charts for study and practice. Remember to download the extra content that comes with this book. It includes lots of bonus practice material—accent exercises, syncopation studies, comping exercises, ostinato patterns, and more!

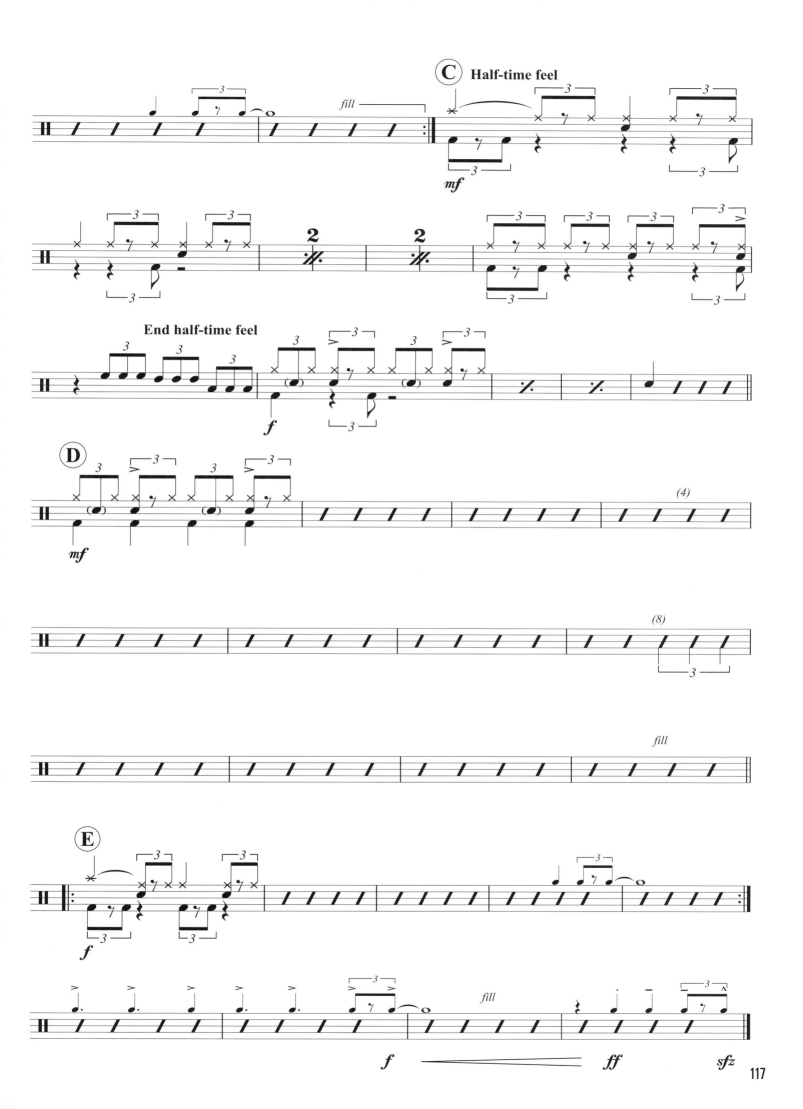

ENCORE #4

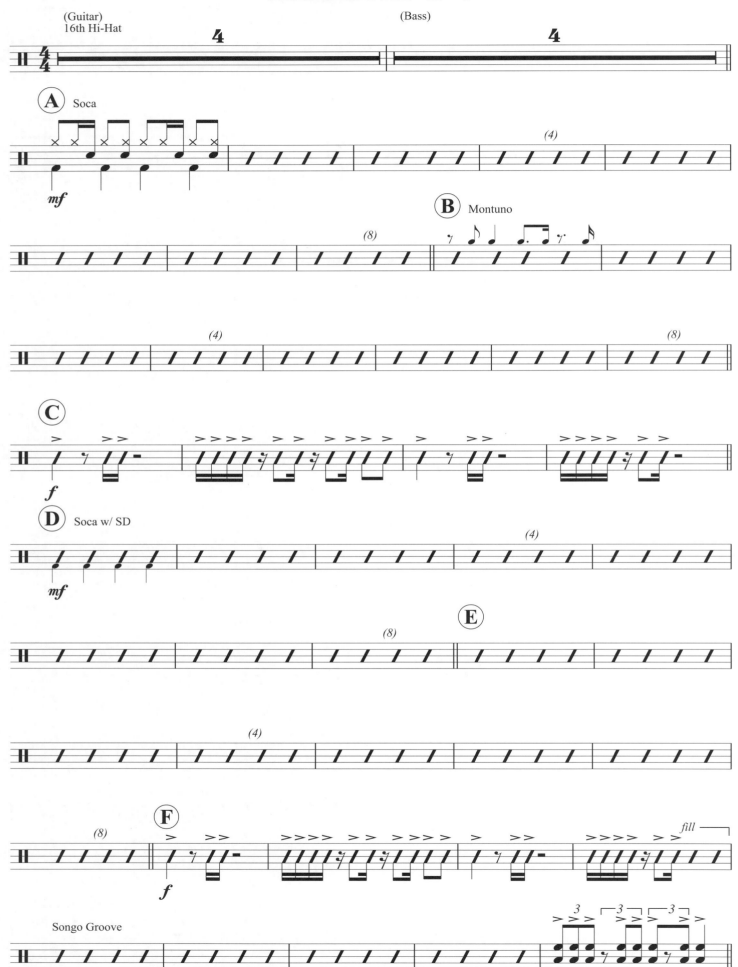

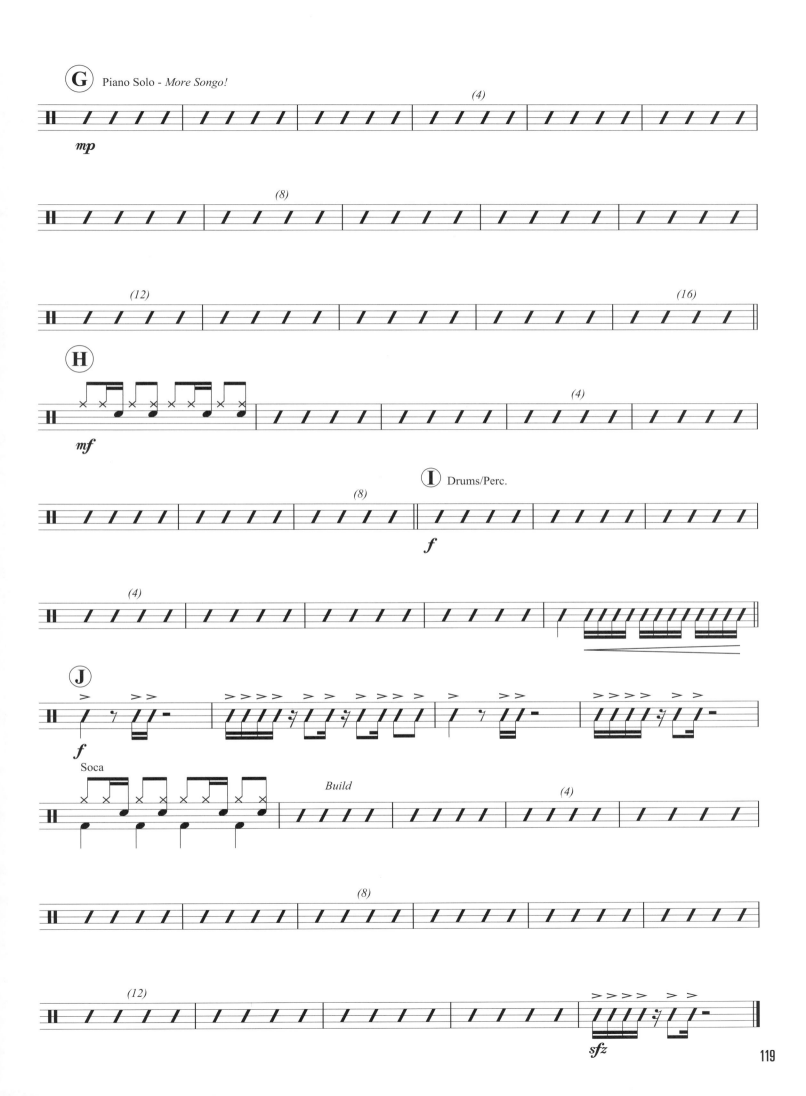

GLOSSARY

A

Accelerando – (*accel.*) Gradually faster, accelerating.

Accent > **–** Play with more emphasis, relative to the marked dynamic level.

Afro-Cuban – The blending of music styles from Africa, Cuba, Puerto Rico, and the Dominican Republic.

Alternate Sticking – Pattern of playing the right and left sticks back and forth in succession (RLRL, etc.)

Articulation – The degree to which notes are separated or connected, such as staccato or legato.

B

Backbeat – Emphasizing the second and fourth beats.

Bar – Also called a measure. The space between bar lines on a staff.

Bar Line – Divides staff into measures, or bars.

Beat – The pulse or counts of a piece of music, denoted by the meter.

Bell – Also called the dome or cup. The raised section of a cymbal immediately surrounding the hole.

Bossa Nova – Popular dance from Brazil.

BPM – Beats per minute. Used to indicate tempo.

Bridge – Transition from one song section to another.

C

Cascara – Afro-Cuban rhythm that is most often played on the shell of a drum.

Calypso – Style of Afro-Caribbean music that originated in Trinidad and Tobago.

Cha-Cha – Afro-Cuban groove that came from a salsa dance known as the cha-cha-cha.

Chorus – Main section of song; usually has the same lyrics each time.

Clave – *Key*: two-measure rhythm that serves as a reference point for all rhythms and melodies found in Cuban music.

Closed Tone – The sound produced when a stick or beater is pressed into the drumhead.

Coda Sign ⊕ **–** Used to end a musical composition. The sign tells you to jump forward to the end section, called a coda.

Comping – Refers to playing "comp"-limentary rhythms with various limbs, usually in the jazz style.

Controlled Stroke – Played by stopping the stick; comprised of the down stroke, tap stroke, and up stroke.

Coordination – The ability to execute multiple rhythms using the hands and feet.

Crescendo – Gradually get louder.

Cross-Stick – Also called side-stick or rim knock. Played by laying stick across drumhead and clicking shaft of stick on the rim.

Cut Time – Also called double time. A time signature in which the half note gets one pulse.

D

D.C. – *Da Capo*: repeat to the beginning.

D.S. – *Dal Segno*: repeat to the D.S. sign 𝄋.

Diminuendo – Gradually get softer.

Dome – Also called the bell or cup. The raised section of a cymbal immediately surrounding the hole.

Dot – Increases the length of a note by adding half of its original value.

Double Bar – Marks the end of a song section.

Double Stroke – Two single strokes played by the same hand (RRLL RRLL, etc.).

Downbeat – The strongest beat in a measure, often the first beat or the quarter-note pulse.

Down Stroke – An element of the controlled stroke, played by stopping the stick two to three inches above the drumhead after impact.

Duple Meter – A common time signature with a basic metrical pattern of two pulses per measure.

Dynamics – Degrees of loudness and softness.

E

Embellishment – Decorating a musical idea by using accents, dynamics, articulations, etc.

F

Feathering – Playing the kick drum very lightly with a quarter-note pulse.

Fermata ⌢ – Symbol indicating to hold a tone or rest beyond the written value, at the discretion of the performer(s).

Fill – Used to "fill-in" space, usually occurring at phrase endings.

Fine – End

First and Second Ending – Repeat the section and substitute the second ending for the first.

Flam – A rudiment made of two notes that almost hit at same time; grace note first then primary note.

Forte *f* – Play loud.

Fortissimo *ff* – Play very loud.

Four on the Floor – Bass drum plays quarter notes on all four beats of a 4/4 measure.

French Grip – Drumming style where the thumbs face upward (as used when playing on the ride cymbal). This technique is very useful when using the fingers for faster playing.

Fulcrum – The specific point where the hand holds the drumstick, usually between the thumb and index finger.

Funk – Music genre that originated in the 1960s when African-American musicians created a rhythmic, danceable type of music that mixed jazz, soul, and R&B music.

G

Ghost Note – Note that is played lightly under the main notes, most often on the snare drum, and typically notated with parentheses.

Grace Note – Small-sized note that is played just slightly before a primary note; possesses no actual time value.

Groove – A persistent repeated rhythmic pattern.

H

Half-Time Feel – This occurs when the backbeat shifts from 2 and 4 to beat 3, creating a new feel.

Hip-Hop – Musical style that started in the 1970s in New York City and became popular world-wide in the 1990s. Some distinct elements include rap, breakdancing, and graffiti art.

House – Type of dance music that grew from the combination of hip-hop and disco.

I

Interpretation – Refers to the drummer's ability of deciding what to play and how when reading a musical chart.

Intro – Beginning section of a song.

Island Music – Refers to music found in the Caribbean region, usually including steel drums.

K

Kick Drum – Term used for bass drum.

L

Legato – Smooth, connected sound.

Long Note – Type of chart notation that calls for a full-value note articulation, commonly played with a cymbal and bass drum (or snare drum) at the same time.

M

Mambo – Recognized as the most popular of all the Afro-Cuban musical styles.

Marcato – ^ *Marked*: short, accented articulation with a "housetop" marking above note.

Matched Grip – Both the right hand and left hand hold the stick the same way, with palms facing down.

Measure – Also called bar. The space between bar lines on a staff.

Meter – The specific time signature for a piece of music. Indicates how many beats per measure and what type of note gets the beat.

Metronome – A device that keeps perfect tempo.

Mezzo Forte *mf* – Play medium loud.

Mezzo Piano *mp* – Play medium soft.

Multi-Measure Rest – Rest for the number of bars indicated.

Musical Form – The layout (construction) of a musical composition (verse, chorus, bridge, etc.).

O

One-Beat Feel – Most often a "fast" or "bright" 3/4 meter with a basic pulse of one beat per measure.

One-Measure Repeat Sign ✗ – Repeat the previous measure.

Open Tone – The sound produced by letting the stick or beater immediately bounce off the drumhead.

Ostinato – Musical figure that is repetitive.

Outro – Ending section of a song.

P

Paradiddle – Sticking pattern that consists of two alternating strokes followed by a double stroke (RLRR LRLL, etc.).

Percussion Clef ‖ – Staff symbol used to indicate non-pitched instruments, such as the drumset.

Pianissimo *pp* – Play very soft.

Piano *p* – Play soft.

R

Rebound Stroke – Relaxed stroke in which the stick is allowed to rebound naturally after hitting the drum.

Rehearsal Mark – Letters or numbers that are usually shown in a box or circle to indicate a different section of music.

Repeat Sign ‖: :‖ – Special bar lines that instruct the player to repeat everything in between them, or repeat back to the beginning.

Rhumba – Popular Cuban dance with a distinct syncopated clave pattern.

Rim Knock – Also called cross-stick and side-stick. Played by laying stick across drumhead and clicking shaft of stick on the rim.

Rimshot – Played by striking the drumhead and rim at the same time.

Ritardando – (*rit.*) *Delaying*, becoming gradually slower.

Rudiments – Basic sticking patterns.

Ruff – Drum rudiment similar to a flam but played with more than one grace note. The stick is allowed to bounce for the grace notes.

S

Salsa – Refers to a form/style of Afro-Cuban music created in the United States in the 1970s. Form usually includes a montuno section with a unique bell pattern.

Samba – The most famous Brazilian musical form. Developed in Bahia and Rio de Janiero during early part of 20th century.

Set-Up – Small fill that leads into an ensemble figure.

Sforzando *sfz* – With sudden force or emphasis.

Short Note – Type of chart notation that calls for a short articulation, commonly played with the snare drum (or bass drum, or even choked hi-hat cymbal) against a standard ride pattern.

Shuffle – A rhythm based off the first and third note of each triplet.

Side-Stick – Also called cross-stick and rim knock. Played by laying stick across drumhead and clicking shaft of stick on the rim.

Single Stroke – One stroke per hand (R L R L, etc.).

Slash Notation – Slash symbols instead of notes on a staff that indicate "time-keeping" in drum parts. Usually means to continue what was previously played for a specified number of beats.

Soca – A high-energy style of music that came from Amercian disco and calypso.

Sock Cymbal – Term used for hi-hat.

Songo – The only Afro-Cuban groove that was conceived on the drumset, as opposed to percussion instruments.

Staccato – · *Detached*: Short, unaccented articulation.

Subdivide – Dividing beats into smaller parts. For example, playing quarter notes while thinking of 8th notes or 16th notes.

Swing Feel – Refers to a rhythmic approach in jazz music, expressed as a triplet division.

Syncopation – The placement of rhythmic accents on upbeats or weak beats.

T

Tap Stroke – An element of the controlled stroke, played from two to three inches above the drumhead, using about a third of a full wrist stroke.

Tempo – The speed at which music is played.

Tenuto – ¯ *Held*: Full value articulation

Three-Beat Feel – Most often used in 3/4 time with a basic pulse of three beats per measure.

Tie – Curved line joining notes together, indicating they are played as one note. Also used to indicate a cymbal should ring out (vibrate), or to show where drum rolls end.

Time – The internal pulse and feel of a drummer; a steady pulsation that is always happening.

Time Signature – Also called meter. Indicates how many beats per measure and what type of note gets the beat.

Trading Fours – Playing four bars of time and then a solo for four bars.

Traditional Grip – Left hand holds stick sideways, right hand holds stick with palm down.

Triple Meter – A common time signature with a basic pulse of three beats per measure.

Tumbao – Repeated rhythm played by the conga player in Afro-Cuban music.

12-Bar Blues – Standard song form for a traditional blues. Three phrases of four bars consisting of the I, IV, and V chords.

Two-Beat Feel – Basic pulse of two beats per measure.

Two-Measure Repeat Sign ² ̸̸. – Repeat the previous two measures.

U

Upbeat – The unaccented beat of a measure. When counting 8th-note rhythms, the "and" in between each number ("1 and 2 and 3 and 4 and").

Up Stroke – An element of the controlled stroke that involves lifting the stick from the butt end (like a small whip motion).

Up-Tempo – Fast

V

Verse – One of the main sections of a song, usually with different lyrics each time.

W

Waltz – A dance written in triple time, where the main pulse (accent) falls on the first beat of each measure.

LISTENING REFERENCES

The listening references below represent some basic examples of the musical styles learned in this book. Each is listed in chronological order so you can trace the development of each style. Please remember this is only a very small sampling and there are so many more you can find. Listen to as much music as you can!

ROCK
Early Rock
Elvis Presley

Chuck Berry

Little Richard

Rockabilly
Jerry Lee Lewis

Stray Cats

Pop, Rock, and Hard Rock
The Beatles

Jimi Hendrix

Eric Clapton

The Rolling Stones

Led Zeppelin

The Doors

Pink Floyd

Aerosmith

Van Halen

Guns N' Roses

Nirvana

Pearl Jam

Soundgarden

JAZZ
New Orleans Second Line
Olympia Brass Hall

Galactic

Dixieland
Louis Armstrong

Preservation Hall Jazz Band

Big Band
Duke Ellington

Gene Krupa

Count Basie

Glenn Miller

Buddy Rich

Brian Setzer

Small Group Jazz
Charlie Parker

John Coltrane

Miles Davis

Thelonious Monk

BLUES
John Lee Hooker

T-Bone Walker

B.B. King

Stevie Ray Vaughan

FUNK
New Orleans Funk
The Meters

Dr. John

The Neville Brothers

"Grease" Funk (ghost notes)
James Brown

Average White Band

Parliament

Tower of Power

Funk Rock

Sly & the Family Stone
Ohio Players
Stevie Wonder
Earth, Wind & Fire
Kool & the Gang
Red Hot Chili Peppers
Dave Matthews Band

Hip-Hop/Rap

The Sugarhill Gang
MC Hammer
N.W.A.
Dr. Dre
Snoop Dogg

Disco

Saturday Night Fever soundtrack
KC and the Sunshine Band
ABBA
Bee Gees

COUNTRY
Western Swing

Bob Wills

Honky Tonk

Hank Williams
Waylon Jennings

Outlaw Country

Johnny Cash
Willie Nelson

Country Rock

Eagles
Marshall Tucker Band

Traditional Country

Patsy Cline
Wynonna Judd

Present Day Bluegrass

Dixie Chicks

Modern Country

Garth Brooks
Rascal Flatts
Tim McGraw

LATIN
Bossa Nova

Antonio Carlos Jobim

Samba

Nana Vasconcelos
Airto Moreira
Sergio Mendes

Cha-Cha

Tito Puente

Soca

Mighty Sparrow

Calypso

Harry Belafonte

Mambo

Tito Puente
Machito

Songo

Michel Camilo
Eddie Palmieri

PERCUSSIVE ARTS SOCIETY INTERNATIONAL DRUM RUDIMENTS

All rudiments should be practiced: open (slow) to close (fast) to open (slow)
and/or at an even moderate march tempo.

I. ROLL RUDIMENTS

A. Single Stroke Roll Rudiments

1. Single Stroke Roll*

2. Single Stroke Four

3. Single Stroke Seven

B. Multiple Bounce Roll Rudiments

4. Multiple Bounce Roll

5. Triple Stroke Roll

C. Double Stroke Open Roll Rudiments

6. Double Stroke Open Roll*

7. Five Stroke Roll*

8. Six Stroke Roll

9. Seven Stroke Roll*

10. Nine Stroke Roll*
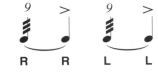

11. Ten Stroke Roll*

12. Eleven Stroke Roll*

13. Thirteen Stroke Roll*

14. Fifteen Stroke Roll*

15. Seventeen Stroke Roll

II. DIDDLE RUDIMENTS

16. Single Paradiddle*

17. Double Paradiddle*

18. Triple Paradiddle

19. Single Paradiddle-Diddle

PAS
www.pas.org

*These rudiments are also included in the original Standard 26 American Drum Rudiments.

Copyright © 1984 by the Percussive Arts Society™, 110 W. Washington St. Suite A, Indianapolis, IN 46204
International Copyright Secured   All Rights Reserved

III. FLAM RUDIMENTS

20. Flam*

21. Flam Accent*

22. Flam Tap*

23. Flamacue*

24. Flam Paradiddle*

25. Single Flammed Mill

26. Flam Paradiddle-Diddle

27. Pataflafla

28. Swiss Army Triplet

29. Inverted Flam Tap

30. Flam Drag

IV. DRAG RUDIMENTS

31. Drag*

32. Single Drag Tap*

33. Double Drag Tap*

34. Lesson 25*

35. Single Dragadiddle

36. Drag Paradiddle #1*

37. Drag Paradiddle #2*

38. Single Ratamacue*

39. Double Ratamacue*

40. Triple Ratamacue*

For information on becoming a member of the Percussive Arts Society™ contact PAS® at:
110 W. Washington St. Suite A, Indianapolis IN 46204 • (317) 974-4488 • E-mail: percarts@pas.org • Web site: www.pas.org

Kennan Wylie holds a Bachelors and Masters degree in Music Education from the University of North Texas. He was an adjunct professor of percussion at University of Arlington for ten years and is currently the percussion instructor at Marcus High School in Flower Mound, Texas. Under his direction since 1990, the Marcus group has received national acclaim both on and off the field. Kennan has authored several books geared toward the teaching of beginning percussion. He has presented clinics throughout the country as well as at the Percussive Arts Society International Convention (PASIC). He is also the past president of the Texas Percussive Arts Society. Wylie plays with the band Fingerprints from the Dallas/Ft. Worth area and is an active freelance musician. He is endorsed by Yamaha Drums, Evans Heads, Innovative Percussion, and Zildjian Cymbals.

Gregg Bissonette is one of the most versatile drummers in the business. Known for his wide range of styles and expertise, he has played with many of the world's leading musicians including Ringo Starr, David Lee Roth, James Taylor, Santana (on his Grammy-award winning album *Supernatural*), Don Henley, Joe Satriani, Andrea Bocelli, ELO, Maynard Ferguson, Spinal Tap, and countless others. He performs regularly in Ringo Starr's All Starr Band. Gregg has also recorded for many films—including *The Bucket List*, *Finding Nemo*, *Best in Show*, *For Your Consideration*, *The Bourne Supremacy*, *The Mighty Wind*, *The Polar Express*, *The Devil Wears Prada*, *Waiting for Guffman*, *Forgetting Sarah Marshall*, *The 40-Year-Old Virgin*—and TV shows, including the hit NBC series *Friends*. He is endorsed by Dixon Drums, Sabian Cymbals, DW, Samson, Remo, Vic Firth, and LP.

A very special thanks to:

Joel McCray – creative audio composition

Bill Bachman – audio engineer

Robert Poole – engraving assistance